The
Super-Helper
Syndrome

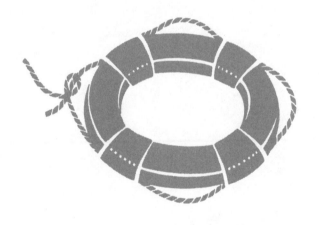

The
Super-Helper
Syndrome

A Survival Guide for Compassionate People

Jess Baker & Rod Vincent

For my Auntie Jean (1931–2020), the woman
who taught me how to like myself.

Every reasonable effort has been made to trace copyright holders and to
obtain their permission for the use of copyrighted material. In the event of
any omission, please contact flint@thehistorypress.co.uk.

Collected Poems and Drawings by Stevie Smith, Faber and Faber Ltd.

Excerpt from *Why Good Things Happen to Good People: The Exciting New
Research That Proves the Link Between Doing Good and Living a Longer, Healthier,
Happier Life* by Stephen Post, Ph.D., copyright © 2007 by Stephen Post, Ph.D.
and Jill Neimark. Used by permission of Broadway Books, an imprint of
Random House, a division of Penguin Random House LLC. All rights reserved.

Siddhartha by Hermann Hesse, Hilda Rosner (trs), Peter Owen Publishers, UK.

Excerpt from *The Upside of Stress: Why Stress Is Good For You, And How To Get
Good At It* by Kelly McGonigal, copyright © 2015 by Kelly McGonigal, PhD.
Used by permission of Avery, an imprint of Penguin Publishing Group, a
division of Penguin Random House LLC. All rights reserved.

First published 2022

FLINT is an imprint of The History Press
97 St George's Place, Cheltenham,
Gloucestershire, GL50 3QB
www.flintbooks.co.uk

British Library Cataloguing in Publication Data.
A catalogue record for this book is available from the British Library.

ISBN 978 0 7509 9886 4

Typesetting and origination by The History Press
Printed and bound in Great Britain by TJ Books Limited, Padstow, Cornwall.

Trees for LYfe

Contents

Authors' Note

A psychotherapist with a pizza trying to connect with a self-harming boy behind his locked bedroom door.

A daughter crying in the car after leaving her screaming mother in a nursing home where she doesn't want to be.

An emergency services operator with a backlog of 520 calls across the region trying to pacify an angry old man waiting for an ambulance for his neighbour.

A social worker searching for accommodation for a client with learning disabilities who had been raped in his home.

These are some of the people we spoke to when we were planning this book. Everyone knows helpers have to cope with traumatic and distressing events. We all know that in addition to the trauma, professional carers typically work prolonged hours with inadequate resources. They face abuse from members of the public or from those in their care. They put themselves in personal danger. And all of this for little monetary reward. During the Covid-19 crisis, their suffering became even more apparent. When Jess spoke to Nicki Credland, chair of the British Association of Critical Care Nurses, she told her that even ICU nurses, who are normally some of the most resilient, have been treated for post-traumatic stress disorder. Instead of one patient per nurse, they suddenly had to look after up to six. She said:

> It's just impossible to give quality care in that environment, so it has caused significant mental health issues in staff – feeling that they are not good enough, not doing their job well enough, not caring for their patients in the way they want to.

Absentee rates among healthcare workers have been at record levels. In the UK's National Health Service, stress now accounts for over 30 per cent of sickness absence, but the problem existed long before the Covid-19 pandemic. In 2002, a US report on 10,000 nurses found that 43 per cent of them had high levels of emotional exhaustion. Unpaid carers are struggling too. There are around 6.5 million in the UK and their numbers have increased in the last couple of years. When 4,500 of them were surveyed in 2020, about 70 per cent reported negative impacts on their physical and mental health.

Deeper down, beneath all of this, there is something else that causes helpers to suffer. It lurks unnoticed. It is not about the challenges or level of trauma they face, though it can make those worse. It drags down everyday helpers and professionals alike and has to do with the very nature of helping. It dwells in the psychology of the helper. That is what this book is about.

This book is based on our experiences as practitioner psychologists and on years of discussing the ideas together. While we have sat side by side in front of a computer screen debating every single word, the concepts originally arose out of Jess's work and are closely interwoven with her own life story. For this reason, we wrote the rest of the book in her voice.

In my early career in the health service and during the last fifteen years as a chartered psychologist, I've had the chance to work with hundreds of helpers. Some of them are in professional caring roles but many are not. Recent clients in my coaching practice have included a geologist, an accountant and a lawyer. Like many of the people you will meet in this book, they were 360-degree helpers. They were looking after others in every aspect of their lives: family, friends, those in their communities and strangers too. All of their jobs required helping as well.

In fact, it is hard to think of any job that doesn't involve helping in some sense or another; perhaps that is the nature of work. How about the supermarket assistant passing down a jar from the top shelf; a festival steward pointing out the camping area; an academic encouraging a self-doubting student; or a boiler engineer replacing a thermostat? Helping is one of the most fundamental human behaviours. Once you start to look for it you find it everywhere: texting to ask how an interview went; setting up a new PlayStation for a friend; pointing a tourist towards the castle; throwing a tennis ball back over the fence. Helping is all around us. It is hard to think of any relationship that doesn't involve it in some way or other. Perhaps that is the nature of life.

This book is about people for whom helping isn't just a vocation; it is a way of life. Here are some of the things they've told me:

> I sometimes feel I've spent my whole life looking after people ... most of what I do in life is about helping ... I feel guilty if I can't help someone ... ever since I was a child, I've done a lot for others... everyone comes to me with their problems.

As I got to know more of these people over time, two themes about their behaviour would not leave me alone. First, their tendency to help can become compulsive. Second, they are so focused on others, they overlook their own needs. I call this the Super-Helper Syndrome – where people feel compelled to help even to the detriment of their own wellbeing. Many of the clients I work with still take on requests for help long after their energies are depleted. They keep going when there is nothing left inside them, and they accept *this* as normal. They are tearful and frustrated by their own limitations to care for other people. They are reluctant to ask for help themselves because they believe their role is to provide. Only when they experience physical manifestations of stress or a state of collapse, do they finally accept help. This book offers practical advice on how to avoid being sucked into the Super-Helper Syndrome in the first place. For anyone who recognises the traits, I also offer ways out of unhealthy patterns of helping. Only by supporting their own mental and physical health can helpers have the strength to care for others in the way they long to.

The ideas in this book first began to take a hazy form nearly twenty years ago, when I was working as a qualitative researcher at Aston University. I lugged cumbersome rolls of flip charts up and down the country to facilitate focus groups with clinical staff to improve the questions in the NHS staff survey. In another project, I designed a stress-management programme as part of a European initiative for healthcare staff, presenting the UK findings in an icy room in the university hospital in Katowice, Poland. During my clinical psychology training, I worked on a project mapping the care of dementia patients in several nursing homes. In all of these settings I witnessed a dedication to helping. And in all of these settings I was alarmed at just how ready the staff were to put their own needs aside. I started to wonder why nobody ever questioned this; why the helpers themselves and everyone else simply accepted it.

The version of the Super-Helper Syndrome in this book comes from thousands of hours of coaching and working with the hundreds of people who have been through my online programmes. That time has given me ample opportunity to define and refine the set of solutions in this survival guide. I've also drawn on research in psychology and neuroscience to elucidate the processes underlying the Super-Helper Syndrome. I have tried to make the research accessible. In doing so, I have dared to draw conclusions from findings that are based on statistical tendencies. These conclusions are always debatable. In the behavioural sciences, especially, for every claim there is a counterclaim. That is the nature of science.

The word 'syndrome' is not meant to imply some sort of medical condition or personality type. I use it in the second sense given in my dictionary: a characteristic combination of opinions, emotions or behaviour. I have never labelled any of my clients as having Super-Helper Syndrome. I have coined the term as a useful moniker for the net effects of compulsive helping and not meeting your own needs. It's a label for a combination of behaviours, not for a person. What I have found, again and again, is that when I describe the concept to people, it resonates with them. Putting a name to a problem can be a relief. It reminds someone that they are not alone. It hints that there is an answer out there. The term Super-Helper Syndrome is for people to self-identify. It's not intended for typecasting others. The last thing I want is yet another label highlighting something wrong with certain groups, especially women, or blaming helpers.

This book is for all helpers, whatever their profession or gender, but I feel I should acknowledge that the majority of people in caring roles are women: 80 per cent of all jobs in adult social care are done by women. In her book, *Invisible Women*, Caroline Criado Perez points out that the majority of unpaid care work is also done by women. According to her, this isn't simply a matter of choice. 'Women's unpaid work is work that society depends on, and is work from which society as a whole benefits,' she writes. The philosopher Kate Manne has exposed how our society obligates women to offer care, affection, emotional support and more. In her book, *Down Girl*, she exposes the expectation that women be 'human givers' rather than human beings. She defines 'feminine coded work' as goods and services, such as care, concern, soothing and nurturing, that women are expected to provide. But I certainly don't want to ignore all the men who are dedicated to helping. Plenty of the examples I've used came from them too. I want this book to be hospitable.

As I mentioned, my own natural habitat is qualitative research. That is the approach I've used to gather real-life examples for this book. Many amazing helpers have shared their experiences in interviews and questionnaires. I've been struck by how much they had to say and how much they were prepared to share. Some of them told me they hadn't been asked about their experience of helping before. Wherever possible I've included their words verbatim. Driven by the principles of qualitative research and my love of NVivo, the data analytics platform, my aim has always been to capture people's perceptions and honour their truth.

I have used the word 'helper' as a generic term. I have sometimes used 'professional carer' to refer to those in paid positions. But I've mostly avoided using 'carer' to describe unpaid helpers, even when they are in long-term helping relationships with someone who is dependent on them. I've done that because, as shown in Chapter 7, one of the ways the Super-Helper Syndrome takes hold is when people find themselves in unhealthy relationships as the 'carer'. Throughout the book I've used the neologism 'helpee' as a catch-all for the person being helped.

The concepts that I have outlined and the examples I've provided do not cover every conceivable possibility. There will always be exceptions; everyone has their own unique set of circumstances. Rather than tie myself in verbal knots trying to cover every eventuality, I offer it all in the spirit that you can take what is useful to you and leave anything that does not apply.

To understand what is going on I start by laying out the working parts of helping – what it really is, how it operates and, crucially, why people want to help at all (Chapters 1 and 2). In the following chapters, you'll find guidance for how helpers can build self-worth (in Chapter 5), keep themselves healthy and look after their own needs (Chapter 9), strengthen resilience and set effective boundaries (Chapter 10). To make any of that possible, we need to counteract the psychology of compulsive helping – that's the main theme of this book (Chapters 4–8). My hope is that if helpers can understand their own thought processes, they won't fall prey to the Super-Helper Syndrome in the first place. By the end, in Chapter 11, I offer a path towards a compassionate life that considers your own story and needs too.

If you are suffering from Super-Helper Syndrome and really want to make some changes in your life, reading can only take you so far – you have to do the work. In each chapter you'll find 'spotlights' that will encourage you to reflect on your own experience, and some exercises to try. In the early part of the book these are aimed at gathering data so that you build up a complete profile of yourself as a helper. Without being too finger-wagging about it, you will get more out of it if you write your answers down. That way you can come back to them in later chapters. By thoroughly exploring your own experience you can achieve change that lasts.

This book is also for the partners, families and friends of helpers, for colleagues and for anyone who manages or trains people in helping roles. As I pointed out just now, it's not in the helper's nature to ask for help. The concepts here can alert you to the signs that someone in your life is vulnerable to the Super-Helper Syndrome and show you how best to support them.

Prologue:
Is Helping in Our Nature?

Helping is all around us – it is an essential and commonplace human behaviour. It's fundamental to our relationships. For some it's a way of life – the very heart of our identity. We help without even thinking about it. Yet, according to many of the world's greatest thinkers, helpers shouldn't even exist. According to them, all human behaviour is essentially selfish. In his book, *The Brighter Side of Human Nature*, Alfie Kohn writes, 'We assume that genuine generosity is only a mirage on an endless desert of self-interest.' Stepping back, it's easy to agree. Much of what we are fed by the media highlights in depressing ways our capacity to do harm to each other – war, violence, crime, the antics of politicians.

The cynical view of humanity has been inherited from some of the great Western philosophers. In 1650, Thomas Hobbes, the granddaddy of modern political thought, wrote that our natural state is to fight each other:

Hereby it is manifest, that during the time men live without a common Power to keep them all in awe, they are in that condition which is called Warre; and such a warre, as is of every man, against every man.

He believed the only way to keep us all in check was the iron fist of a leviathan state.

Bernard Mandeville, the Dutch social philosopher, even went so far as to claim that society couldn't function if we weren't selfish and corrupt. In his satirical poem, *The Grumbling Hive*, a colony of bees decide to live honest, good lives, but sadly this leads to the ultimate collapse of their hive; 'Such were the Blessings of that State; Their Crimes conspired to make 'em Great.'

Frederick Nietzsche, whose depiction of the *Übermensch* has been used to inspire and justify totalitarians and fascists, would probably take a dim view of a book about the Super-Helper Syndrome (the Überhelper?). He goes beyond merely thinking that our nature is flawed and that we survive only by strength. In his most famous work, *Thus Spoke Zarathustra*, his alter ego attacks one of the main themes of this book: compassion. I am appalled, but can't contain my hollow laugh as I quote:

> Truly, I do not like them, the compassionate who are happy in their compassion: they are too lacking in shame. If I must be compassionate, I still do not want to be called compassionate; and if I am compassionate then it is preferably from a distance.

Of course, there have been philosophers who have taken a more forgiving view, for example David Hume and Immanuel Kant. More recently, in his book *Enlightenment Now*, Steven Pinker sets out a smorgasbord of data to suggest humanity is gradually making things better. He laments the continued influence of Nietzsche in the twenty-first century, when such ideas had already inspired two world wars. The political philosopher Kristen Renwick Monroe recounts inspiring stories of philanthropists, heroic helpers and rescuers from the Holocaust. For her, at least some of our behaviour is purely altruistic: when we take on a different way of seeing things – the altruistic perspective. According to her, 'Where the rest of us see a stranger, altruists see a fellow human being.'

In science, too, a negative view has often come out on top. Altruism presented a conundrum for evolutionary biology, which explained the development of humanity as a series of random mutations. And as with Nietzsche's philosophy, people have used Charles Darwin's discoveries to justify violent or competitive behaviour. The over-enthusiastic parent on the touchline who yells, 'Come on Tarquin, smash his head in!', might defend this by claiming, 'It's survival of the fittest.' But Tarquin's dad has only a partial view of evolutionary theory. *Fitness*, as Darwin coined it in *On the Origin of Species*, actually refers to survival of the *most fit*. In other words, organisms with the best fit to their environment will survive. While *fitting* the environment does frequently call for strength, aggression or competitiveness, it can indicate the need for nurturing behaviours too. That can be seen in behaviours like the instinct in orangutan mothers to nurse their young for up to seven years, longer than any other mammal. Evolutionary biologists developed theories of kin selection to explain behaviour like this. They also came up with 'reciprocal altruism' (the idea that there is a pay-off in return for helping behaviours). This allowed them to provide an explanation for apparently altruistic acts, such as drongo birds warning meerkats of an eagle overhead, without letting go of the essential underlying selfishness implied by the theory of natural selection.

When Richard Dawkins released *The Selfish Gene* in the 1970s, it gave everyone yet another excuse to claim that all behaviour is self-seeking. Now we were at the mercy of evil genes, bent only on replicating themselves down the centuries. Dawkins believed that if we want to act unselfishly, we will get little help from our biology; because we are born selfish, 'We are survival machines – robot vehicles blindly programmed to preserve the selfish molecules known as genes'. Recently I had to buy the fortieth anniversary edition of Dawkins' book because my treasured and heavily annotated copy of the original paperback was lost in a house move. There is a hint of backspacing in the epilogue to the new edition. Dawkins stresses that genes actually repeatedly meet and cooperate with others as they troop through the generations. He goes so far as to say, 'the cooperative gene might have been an equally appropriate title for the book'. That gives us hope that helping has some genetic roots (as we will see later).

Economists, too, have not given humanity much credit. They have often considered what appears to be altruism as a good. Not a good thing (which it obviously is), but a commodity that is bought and sold. In other words, we will only help if there is some sort of pay-off, either material or psychological. That type of reward, for example feeling good because you helped someone, is called 'psychic utility'. The concept of reciprocity is therefore important for economists as well as biologists when it comes to accounting for altruism. And it is important to us because reciprocity is a fundamental dynamic in helping relationships, whether you believe in altruism or not – I'll come back to it in Chapter 2.

Adam Smith is probably the greatest economist to have written about human nature. His early explorations of sympathy are strikingly similar to modern research into how empathy motivates helping behaviour, another topic we will look into. But strangely, he takes both sides of the argument, one in each of the two books he published. In *The Wealth of Nations* he claims that mankind is essentially selfish, but in *The Theory of Moral Sentiments* he acknowledges that we have something in our nature that gives us an interest in the happiness of others, even if we receive nothing in return, 'except the pleasure of seeing it'. Apparently, German economists have labelled this contradiction 'das Adam Smith Problem'.

In my own territory, psychologists too have been lured towards the darker side. Sigmund Freud believed our actions fall out of a combination of unconscious selfish drives and trying to protect our ego. These days social psychologists do research 'prosocial behaviour', but even this was precipitated by striking examples of a lack of helping, the most famous of which was when *The New York Times* reported that thirty-eight people ignored the cries of Kitty Genovese when she was murdered in public in 1964.

The most prominent researcher has been Daniel Batson. He set out on a thirty-year quest to disprove the existence of altruism. In his most famous experiment, students at Princeton Theological Seminary had to prepare a talk, then walk to another building to give the talk. On the way they passed a groaning man slumped in an alleyway. The experimenters found that those who were in a hurry were less likely to stop and help, even if they were on the way to give a talk on the subject of the Good Samaritan. Some of the seminarians even stepped over the groaning man.

So where does all this leave us? What if all those philosophers, economists, biologists and psychologists were right? What if the vast majority of human behaviour really is driven by egoistical motives? That is easy enough to believe. Just look at today's headlines. If the prevailing view of Western thought has been that altruism is impossible, or at the very least extremely unlikely, what does that say about the helpers I meet? Perhaps it suggests that they are rare; that there are a relatively small number of people who do the lioness's share of the caring. And if that is the case, then it is hardly surprising that they are overburdened. It is hardly surprising that they take on more than they can handle. It is hardly surprising that they sink into the Super-Helper Syndrome.

It suggests we need to help them survive.

Part One

The Art
of Helping

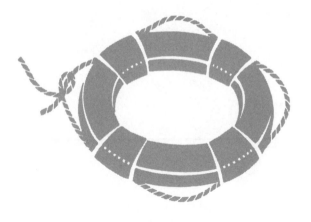

Chapter 1

How Can I Help?

Isn't it ever so slightly preposterous how little instruction we get for the things that matter most in life? You're just expected to know how to be a good romantic partner – there is no training programme. You wake up one day to find yourself the parent of a teenager but you didn't sit the exam. You arrive at work and you are told you are leading a team but the only role models you've had were bad managers. More examples keep coming to mind. What about resolving conflicts or managing money? What about helping?

We have seen how commonplace the act of helping is but hardly any of us set out to analyse it. There are surprisingly few books that directly address the question of what it means to help or how to do it well. Even people in the caring professions are given less training in the art of helping than you would think. The emphasis is on teaching technical skills, which are essential but not enough on their own. If we carefully dismantle helping and lay out all the working parts on the table, we can better understand why it sometimes goes wrong. This will also give us a shared language to talk about the Super-Helper Syndrome. By the end of this chapter, we should have some answers to questions like:

Why don't people take the advice I give them?
Is it possible to help by doing nothing?
Are good intentions enough?

If you don't know what impact you've had, is it still helping?

Is self-help help?

Does giving help make people dependent?

What is the single biggest mistake people make when trying to help?

So, What Exactly is Help?

The place to start is the dictionary. Help is defined by the *Oxford Dictionary of English* as making it 'easier or possible for (someone) to do something by offering them one's services or material aid'. What I like about that definition is that it includes the word 'offering'. That allows room for some sort of negotiation and the possibility of the helpee refusing. Personally, I would like the definition to go further and explicitly state that it only qualifies as help when it is wanted. And there is too much emphasis there on doing. The definition above describes making it easier for someone to *do something*; but you can help someone to just *be*. That is not semantic nit-picking. As we will see when we look at the different forms of help, supportive help is often neglected. Therapists help people to just *be*: be calmer, be more accepting of themselves. Going back to the dictionary, surely there is more to helping than 'services or material aid'. What about sympathy, compassion or love? Supportive help is overlooked again.

Here is an alternative definition for our purposes:

Make something easier or possible for someone by offering them resources, information, expertise and, or, support, when they both want and need this.

The Four Forms of Help

This alternative definition goes beyond the one in the dictionary to spell out the 'services or material aid' that are being offered. Help always appears in these four forms: resources, information, expertise and support. Whenever we help someone, we offer one or more of these. If you cast your eyes back a few pages, you'll find the supermarket assistant offering resources help in reaching for the jar, and the friend offering expert help in setting up the PlayStation. In fact, you will find two of each of the four forms of help.

When helping goes wrong, the chances are it's because the wrong form of help has been offered. There's a mismatch between the expectations of the helper and the expectations of the helpee. Imagine you call a friend to offload distress about your autocratic boss. Angry on your behalf, they squawk on about how you could find another job tomorrow with your qualifications and experience. They say you should tell them to stick it (information help). At the end of the call, you mumble all you wanted was a sympathetic ear (supportive help).

Taking a closer look at the four forms reveals a lot about what works and what doesn't in different helping scenarios. As we go through them, think about which of the four forms you most naturally give. By doing this you can start to build up a picture of your own individual style as a helper. This can also reveal how vulnerable you might be to the Super-Helper Syndrome.

Help Form 1: *Resources Help – The Edge of Husbandry*

Are you constantly doing things for other people? Do you lend belongings that are never returned? Are you the first to reach for the bill? If so, you are like many of those I interviewed for this book. They were generous-hearted and free with their possessions. However, for helpers, having something is frequently associated with feeling guilty for having it. People with Super-Helper Syndrome who have a resource feel obliged to offer it to anyone who doesn't. And once they start, they go on dishing out their resources like someone at a conveyor belt piping salted caramel fondant into chocolates.

When I analysed the data, the interviewees and questionnaire respondents were providing seven categories of resources: labour, status, space, tools, materials, data and finances. In addition to the overall obligation to give or lend resources, each of these categories sets its own traps. While I whizz through them, you might recognise your own helping tendencies. By labour I mean the most obvious type of resource, doing things for people. They were carrying in the shopping, driving neighbours to the doctor, ordering online groceries for elderly relatives and a multitude of other things. They were invariably squeezed by time. When they weren't doing things themselves, they were supplying labour, as in, 'I sent my son round to do that for her.' They supplied other resources too. A common example was allowing access to their own status or attributes by proxy, as in, 'I put in a good word for him with the HR director.' Examples of providing space included storing an antique table in the garage so they couldn't park their own car and allowing a friend to sleep on the sofa. There were several instances of helpers who had let someone else into their home but couldn't get rid of them. The category of tools, materials and data included everything from umbrellas to clothes to books, even a van, as well as what we typically think of as tools, like a screwdriver.

Offering material resources brings up the question, do you want the resource returned and, if so, in what condition? Natural helpers aren't good at protecting their own rights when they provide resources. And other people can be only too happy to take advantage of this.

Several of the interviewees talked about the frustration of getting things back late, damaged or not at all. When I was 15, I borrowed a bag of psychology books from my friend's mum. I carted them around all summer to read on buses and in the park. When I handed them back, she took one out and caressed the scuffed cover, smoothing her fingers over the dog-eared pages. The others were the same. She was appalled. I still feel guilty about not looking after them as well as she'd expected.

> Neither a borrower nor a lender be,
> For loan oft loses both itself and friend,
> And borrowing dulleth th' edge of husbandry.
> Shakespeare, Polonius in Hamlet, Act 1, Sc. 3

With finances help, the question of how to get the resources back is even more fraught. Money is emotive enough, even when we aren't lending or giving it away. Just thinking about it makes many of us uneasy. People with Super-Helper Syndrome buy presents they can't afford. They frequently lend money that is never repaid. In the end this leads to snowballing resentment and, as Polonius points out to his son who is heading off to college in *Hamlet*, it can even destroy friendships. Whether you agree with him or not, perhaps it's a sound principle to write the money off in your head as soon as it leaves your wallet.

If you do hope to get your resources back, it's important to clarify your expectations by contracting. If you find that difficult, you are not alone. We'll come back to asserting boundaries. For now, contracting simply means agreeing in advance that you do want this back, when you want it back and in what condition you want it back.

Help Form 2: *Information Help – L'help quotidien*

I've just got back from Price's bakery. As I left the house, Rod called out, 'Don't forget the eggs for Lilly's cake.' On my way up the hill I caught up with a neighbour to let her know her handbag was hanging open. She thanked me and told me the street barbecue has been confirmed for Saturday. I said I would do marinated kebabs, she said she would bring a big bowl of her creamy coleslaw. I waited at the kerb until a driver waved me across. At the bakery, Mrs Price said the sourdough was just out of the oven. As she was wrapping the loaf, she told me they would be closed Thursday. My phone vibrated. It was a text from Lucy: 'the blue boar says ok for meeting next week'. I came back into the house and took one look at Rod sifting cocoa into flour. 'Shit! I forgot the eggs.'

Information help is where you provide someone else with useful knowledge. In contrast with giving away resources, with this form of help you still have the information yourself after you have given it to someone else. For example, telling someone about a book you enjoyed rather than giving them your own copy. With information help you don't run the risk of your resources being depleted. That's one advantage for the helper – information is cheap. Of all the squillions of instances of help that go on every day around the world, information help is the most common. It's so ubiquitous it goes unnoticed. Almost every conversation involves sharing information. In my fifteen-minute trip to the bakery above, I can find ten examples.

Information help is at the core of how we use language. There's advising, explaining, giving feedback, notifying, storytelling and reminding. It can even be non-verbal, like sign language or the guy in the car who waved me across the road to the bakery. It's how we learn just about everything important we know. It is the currency of schools and colleges. Teaching makes use of another advantage of this form of help: you can pass on information to a group of people at the same time. On the other hand, communication is notoriously tricky: you never know if you have been fully understood. Often you aren't around to see whether someone implements your advice or to find out if it worked. With information help, you can't always know if you have done the recipient any good. What's more, because information is cheap, it has other disadvantages from the point of view of the helpee. They have to filter out the false, the fake, the advertising, the propaganda.

Remember your friend squawking at you to quit your job, and how that is an example of giving information help when supportive help is what's wanted? On the desk beside me there is a copy of *Helping* by MIT psychologist Edgar Schein, one of the few books I could find on the subject. Professor Schein provides twenty-six examples of what he calls the 'Many Forms of Help'. But going through his list, fifteen of them fall into my category of information help. Specifically, nine of them are advice. Schein gives only two examples of supportive help (even professors of psychology overlook this). That's an easy oversight: readily giving advice is the default form of help for many of us. It's a particular temptation if you have a compulsion to help.

Information help isn't just about passing on facts or advice. There's sharing insights too. Sparking self-discovery is one of the most rewarding parts of being a coach. When people understand their own motives and underlying beliefs it leads to breakthrough moments. So, information help is one of the most quotidian forms of help but can also be one of the most powerful.

Help Form 3: *Expert Help – Can You Just Take a Quick Look at ...*
People who are prone to Super-Helper Syndrome are drawn to jobs where they provide expert help. They are found in health and social care, in professional services and any workplace where they can help.

The defining feature of this form of help is that an expert does something that the helpee doesn't know how to do, unlike resources help when they know how to do something but simply don't have the time or the where-withal. Obvious examples are a surgeon repairing a hernia, an engineer servicing an alarm system or a techie removing a virus. Qualifications or authorisation come to mind when we think about expert help, but they are by no means always necessary. Remember this is about the form of help being given, not about who is doing the helping. If someone we consider to be an expert on a subject is teaching another person about that subject, that's information help. Anyone doing something for someone else that they don't know how to do for themselves is giving expert help, whether or not we might think of them as an 'expert'. When you block a spam number from a colleague's mobile phone or tune a guitar for a friend who's just started to learn, that's expert help. A lot of what we do for young children, such as tying up their shoelaces, is expert help.

He who does not know one thing knows another.

African Proverb

Now that we've differentiated exactly what it is, we can look at the advantages and disadvantages of this form of help. Expert help can be essential and even lifesaving, but it comes with several risks. Many of these relate to the fact that giving expert help is doing something for someone, or to someone, and it's usually easier for the helper to just get on with it. In fact, one reason for choosing to give expert help in the first place is that it's quicker to do something yourself than to show someone how to do it for themselves. Unlike with information help, experts don't pass on their knowledge. The helpee is none the wiser after the event. That's fine in some situations – I don't need to know how to repair my own hernia – but, in others, it creates unnecessary dependency. If a parent keeps on tying their child's shoelaces, the child never learns. For this reason, it's worth considering whether another form of help is more appropriate before offering expert help.

Usually, expert help works better when it is blended with the other forms. In their urgency, professional experts sometimes overlook the need for information or support. The helpee wants more than just something done for them. The engineer could tell the customer how to reset the intruder alarm. Sometimes it's important to give information as a form of support. A healthcare professional might talk you through a procedure to reassure you that everything is going okay.

Another type of risk has to do with the level of responsibility attached to this form of help; the expert is to blame if it all goes wrong. It is one more reason to think about the forms of help you offer. It's also the reason the global professional indemnity insurance industry is worth nearly 40 billion dollars.

Giving expert help can put the helper in a position of power. There is a risk that the helpee feels inadequate or vulnerable in the hands of an expert, or that the expert might abuse their power.

Finally, the biggest risk for experts who are also compulsive helpers ... as much as they love their friends and family, they get inundated with requests to apply their skills for free. There were many examples from the interviews. One dentist was at a party where a woman cornered her in the kitchen and pulled her cheek back asking her to take a look at a chipped tooth. The dentist said she grabbed the torch in her handbag without thinking.

Help Form 4: *Supportive Help – The Heart of Helping*
Empathising, encouraging, reassuring, consoling and soothing are a different kind of help from the other three forms we've explored. Supportive help is the odd one out because it doesn't necessarily solve the problem; it makes the problem easier to cope with. When it's the principal form of help, supportive help works by facilitating someone to solve their own problem. It's about showing the helpee that they already have the resources, information or expertise to help themselves. Commonly, it's required in addition to the other forms of help. Support is the steel joist that underpins the other forms. You can't always see it, but it reinforces them.

For some of us, supportive help is the most rewarding form of help to give. But as we've seen, it is often neglected. There are times when all the helpee wants is a listening ear, but it's tempting to jump to solution mode – to start squawking. That's why it can be one of the most skilled and demanding forms of help. But sadly, it is underrated or seen as nebulous, rather than as a means of tangible results. Management trainers call it a soft skill. But it's vital. Louis Penner of the Cancer Institute at Wayne State University studied children with acute lymphocytic leukaemia attending outpatient clinics. He found that children whose parents showed greater 'empathic concern' experienced less pain and suffering during treatments such as lumbar punctures. Those parents tended to protect and comfort their children more. They also engaged in 'normalising' behaviours such as playing with their children, chatting to them or reading to them during the procedures. This kind of research shows the value of supportive help.

Supportive help comes in many guises. It can be purely non-verbal, such as smiling and nodding to show understanding, or murmuring your concern. It can also be physical, hugging someone or stroking their arm. It can actually be passive – just sitting by the bedside. Although it's nice to know, you don't always have to know that you are helping, to help; it still fits the definition we discussed.

Occasionally support can even be helping by inaction. For example, if a child wants to reorganise their bedroom with their own collection of knick-knacks and posters, their parent might be tempted to get involved. Depending on the situation, it can be more helpful to do nothing. If the parent holds back, the child has more opportunity to express themselves and take ownership of the end result.

Supportive help relies heavily on the quality of the relationship. It typically requires personal disclosure which can leave the helpee feeling vulnerable. At a crisis point in my own life, I spent a couple of years in psychotherapy. Before I met the therapist I could work with, I had two sessions with another woman. When I arrived for the second one, she said, 'Before we start, can I ask what colour eyeshadow you are wearing and where you get your hair cut?' That was after I had spent much of the first session disclosing issues about appearance and identity. An important element of effective supportive help is to foster an atmosphere of mutual trust so both of you feel safe.

Supportive help demands a different mix of skills from the other forms of help. The most critical of those is listening. Stillness and patience play a part too: giving the helpee time to talk and allowing space for silence. Not everyone is good at this. Using these skills might seem passive to an onlooker, but they do take a great deal of internal control. To give supportive help is to give something of yourself and that comes at an emotional cost. And it expends energy. These are risks for compassionate people.

Spotlight 1.1: *How I Help*

Think about the four forms of help: resources, information, expert, supportive. Which of them come most naturally to you in the various aspects of your life? Make a note of your answers to the following questions:

Which forms of help do you tend to give at work?

Which forms of help do you tend to give in your personal life?

Which forms of help do you rarely give?

Try to see if there's a pattern as this will give you a sense of how you position yourself as a helper. There are no right or wrong answers. You might find you tend to give one particular form of help or that you give all four. At this stage you are just trying to build more awareness of yourself as a helper.

As well as thinking about your own helping style in Spotlight 1.1, you might consider what help you receive from your community, colleagues, friends or family. What help do you ask for, and what do you need? Do different people offer you different things? In my life there are certain people I would turn to for resources but would never go to for support, and vice versa.

Skilled helpers balance the four forms of help like a sound engineer at a mixing desk. They enhance their expert help by increasing their level of support where it's needed. They discern when a helpee really needs resources. They're able to efficiently switch to giving information. As well as making use of the subtle interplay of all four forms, skilled helpers instinctively know how the following three key dynamics play out in different helping situations.

Help Dynamic 1: *Autonomy vs. Dependency – Teach a Man to Fish and then You Don't Have to Give Him a Fish*

The first distinction is between whether the helpee is equipped to solve their own problems in the future versus having to repeatedly come back for assistance. Psychologists who study prosocial behaviour have labelled this distinction autonomy-oriented versus dependency-oriented help. It matters to us because a common feature of the Super-Helper Syndrome is that you can become embroiled in relationships where people are dependent on your help.

> I was the only mum on the PTA who worked full time. Typical me. I started off assisting the treasurer with the finances, then she left, so I was thrown into that role, and then the chair left so I take over that and I find myself doing a dual role managing everything – that was interesting for three and a half years [rolls eyes]. Sometimes you help so much that everyone just gets used to you doing it all.
>
> Accountant, Interviewee

When I am coaching people, I try to leave them with tools and techniques to be self-sufficient in the longer term (autonomy oriented). But I do offer a brief emergency call as part of the contract. When clients take me up on that, my job is to bring them down off the ceiling or pick them up from the floor. In those calls I'm more likely to give direct advice or short-term coping strategies (dependency oriented). Both types of help have value if they are congruous with what people need in that moment.

Creating autonomy isn't always easy. A common experience of coaches is what I call the therapy-go-round. At first the client turns up glazed with enthusiasm. In every session after that they want to be reminded of what was said before. The coach – desperate to help – tries numerous strategies. The therapy-go-round client dismisses any hint that they might come up with their own ideas. They agree to the coach's recommendations but don't take any action. They turn up week after week. Eventually they begin to express disappointment that they haven't got more out of the sessions. It's a shame. They do need help but all they are able to do at this stage is maintain a dependency-oriented relationship.

31

Thinking back to the four forms of help, they are autonomy oriented or dependency oriented to varying degrees. This is worth considering when you look at the forms of help you typically give. Expert help is essentially dependency oriented. Offering resources also invites dependency, as in the famous fishing example referenced in this section's heading. One of the advantages of information help is that it is more likely to promote independence. Supportive help is a subtle game. On the face of it, it's autonomy oriented because it's about enabling someone to solve their own problems, but it can morph into a dependent relationship, as in the therapy-go-round, or be subject to the helper's motives: do they genuinely want to create autonomy?

Spotlight 1.2: *Increasing Autonomy*

Looking back at your responses to Spotlight 1.1:

Are the forms of help that you tend to give more autonomy or dependency oriented?

Who are the people in your life that depend on your help?

How much control do you have over the extent to which they depend on you?

Are there ways you could reduce their long-term dependency on you?

Again, in this spotlight, you are just making notes on your own experience. Clients of mine, when thinking about the third question, often believe they have no control at all. They feel overwhelmed by the demands of so many people. At this stage, I'm encouraging you to become aware of the dynamics of your helping relationships. We'll tackle how to change the dynamics later.

Help Dynamic 2: *Assumptive vs. Responsive Help – I was Only Trying to Help*

Can you remember a time when you offered advice that wasn't appreciated? Have you ever been turned down when you volunteered to do something? In situations like these it is sometimes because the offer of help was what social psychologists call 'assumptive' rather than 'responsive' help. All helping falls into one or the other of these categories. Assumptive help wasn't asked for; responsive help was. This distinction is important for us because it can be the reason why helping works or doesn't. It is also revealing about the personality characteristics of people who are susceptible to Super-Helper Syndrome.

It's easy to rush to the conclusion that responsive help takes the prize over assumptive help. At least, when they ask, you know the person wants something. But it's not quite that simple. It's true that assumptive help does have risks. Information help is characteristic of this – we love giving advice, even when it's not asked for, but we hate taking advice. As a parent we struggle to hold back rather than solving a child's every difficulty. It's a tough call to weigh up the damage of letting them make their own mistakes against the damage to your long-term relationship if you keep intervening. Assumptive help risks not being help at all, according to our definition, which included 'when they both want and need this'. The other day on BBC *Woman's Hour* I heard a disabled woman tell the presenter how, when she is waiting at a kerb, strangers assume they can help. They grab her wheelchair, shunt her across the road and dump her on the other side without even speaking to her.

That doesn't make assumptive help sound too appealing, so let's rebalance things. Sometimes it is the right sort of help. There are times when people can't ask for help. If your friend is about to crash into the back of another car it is okay to yank on the handbrake. There are times when people won't ask for help. For us, Patrick was the perfect next-door neighbour. While he was still able to, he frequently ferried people to and from the airport. He took in our parcels, watered the garden when we were away and drove us out to the forest so we could take a long walk back home. He would always stay late at our parties. He was the sort of person who would help others but would never ask for help himself. As a proud man, in the last year or two of his life, despite being seriously ill, he still wanted to be self-sufficient. We knew he had a series of hospital appointments to periodically drain fluid from his lung. We also knew that he would be too stubborn to call an ambulance and would attempt to drive himself. When Rod offered him a lift, he politely refused. He gently repeated his offer until Patrick graciously accepted. Assumptive help like that requires a delicate and timely approach. We were acutely aware of this and debated at length whether to offer in the first place and which of us should make the offer.

Spotlight 1.3: *The Assumptive Trap*

Can you think of any instances when:

You offered assumptive help where it wasn't needed and/or wanted?

Assumptive help was needed but you didn't offer it?

If you have a lot of examples in answer to the first question, then this can be a sign of compulsive helping, so it would be something to bear in mind when we come to looking at that. Alternatively, if you have more examples for the second question, then this can be related to assertiveness, which is a key topic for helpers and something discussed in Chapter 10.

One of the challenges of supporting people suffering from Super-Helper Syndrome is that they seldom ask for help for themselves. So, if you want to help them, assumptive help may be your only choice.

I was much too far out all my life
And not waving but drowning.

Stevie Smith, 'Not Waving but Drowning'

Even when someone asks for your help, you don't always know exactly what they need. With responsive help it can feel like you are downing your pen with five minutes to spare at the end of the exam and then you realise you have misread the question. The most common way that helping goes wrong is when the solution doesn't properly match the problem. It's the classic script played out between customers and suppliers, turning the relationship sour. The customer says, 'You haven't done what I wanted.' The supplier replies, 'You didn't tell me what you wanted.' The sections above aimed to clarify the risks of giving the wrong form of help. Even when responding to a specific request, in all but the simplest circumstances, it's crucial to ask questions. In more open-ended helping relationships it is essential to thoroughly explore the request for help before responding. That way, together with the helpee, you can avoid the biggest mistake, pinpoint what they really need and involve them in defining a solution.

Helpful Questions

There are various categories of questions that can be used to discern how best to help:

Fact gathering
What's the history of this situation? How did they get here? What's really going on? Who else is involved? What have they tried so far?

Exploring their viewpoint
How are they feeling about the situation? What do they want to happen? What do they need to achieve it? What form of help would they like? How can you help?

Identifying alternatives
What are their options? Would they like you to suggest more options? Who else needs to be involved?

Discussing practicalities
What resources do they already have (e.g. time, money, contacts)? Who's going to do what? When will they start? When does it need to be done by? What involvement is required from you?

Help Dynamic 3: *High vs. Low Status – Who's Got the Power?*

One of the reasons people don't ask for help is what the social psychologist Edgar Schein refers to as the 'one-downness' of needing help. When you ask for help you are admitting you have a need that the other person doesn't have. You are acknowledging they may have the power to remedy this. Our neighbour, Patrick, may have been refusing help to avoid that sense of one-downness. According to Schein, 'Needing help often feels demeaning. In US culture, the quip is often heard "Real men don't ask for directions"'. That does sound familiar, but Schein goes further. He claims that in cultures like the US, there is a stigma attached to admitting 'that one uses servants of various sorts'. That claim sounds strange to me: the person hiring domestic help has all the money and power. I am reminded of the documentary *The Helper* about foreign domestic workers. Those women, mainly from the Philippines, leave their own homes and children to work in Hong Kong, looking after the homes and children of other people. They work six days a week, for minimal wages, sending most of it back home. They don't see their own children for years. Crying to camera, it's clear those women do not feel one up.

It is easy to think of other examples where the helper can be one-down or vulnerable – shop assistants, hotel staff and health-service workers immediately come to mind. I am perplexed by Schein's summary that in every helping relationship, 'The client is one-down and therefore vulnerable; the helper is one-up and therefore powerful'.

Although I agree that helping relationships create a power imbalance, I prefer to think in terms of the more fluid concept of status: sometimes the person asking for help is in a lower-status position, but sometimes it is the other way around. It depends on the context of the help being requested, the role of the helper and the personalities involved. Status can also be a function of the social game they are playing. A few years ago, I trained in improvisation drama. In the Christmas Party Game, we learned to switch alternately between high and low status, playing either a company CEO or the company cleaner. It is remarkable how, when trying to act as the high-status cleaner, just by using your physical demeanour and tone of voice you can gain power.

Status is a key dynamic in all helping relationships. It's a dynamic worth considering whenever you set out to help people. As we've seen, a perceived loss of status can hold people back from asking for help. On the other side of the pair of scales, a lack of status for helpers creates enormous challenges in stressful care situations and can make a difficult job even more difficult.

By now we have answered all of the questions listed at the start of this chapter apart from one: is self-help help? My answer is yes, yes yes! If you are happy with my definition, then *you* can be the 'someone' who benefits from your own help. That's the whole point of this book – to show helpers how to help themselves.

Chapter 2

Love or Money?

Understanding what motivates helping will allow us to go on to explore why it can become compulsive. So, how do people make the decision whether or not to help? You might not believe it, but a group of scientists have come up with the following formula:

$$M \times (D \times (1 + B_{self}) + K \times B_{recipient} + C_{inaction}) > C_{action}$$

Don't worry, there's no need to memorise it! But the SAVE formula does sum up a vast body of research from the field of prosocial behaviour. It is also a neat compilation of everything going on backstage when you decide whether or not to help. It includes the sociocultural context (M) and whether that encourages or discourages helping. It considers whether you are a natural helper (D). Then there is K, the helper's biases about the helpee, such as whether they are part of the same group. $B_{recipient}$ stands for how much benefit the helpee will get and B_{self} what is in it for the helper. And finally, the costs of helping, C_{action}, versus $C_{inaction}$, the costs of not helping, such as guilt or public shame.

When I first came across this I did wonder if the very idea of a formula is academic navel-gazing gone too far. If you're questioning whether such a thing could have any use in the real world, you might be interested to know that one of the scientists who developed it was Aleksandr Kogan. He's the guy who was hauled up before Parliament to explain his involvement in developing the algorithms used by Cambridge Analytica to influence voting intentions in the US and the UK. Alongside his research at Cambridge University, Kogan, who also went by the name of Dr Spectre, set up several companies to develop consumer insights by harvesting big data from social media. Who knows what fiendish uses this formula could be put to? Perhaps androids will require an algorithm to instruct their artificially intelligent brains to either initiate paramedic mode or just step over your body. But back to humans and why we help. I want to draw your attention to only one of the terms in the formula, B_{self}: what is in it for the helper.

What do you think is the main reason you help? I ask this because it is the key question for anyone who has experienced Super-Helper Syndrome. Our true motives are complex and sometimes hidden; later we will explore them in depth. To get us closer, we will first have a look at the question of whether people get something in return for their help.

Reciprocity – You Pick My Peaches and I'll Pick Yours

Have you ever been in a friendship where you made all the effort – keeping in touch, suggesting meeting up, sending well-wishes? It's unsettling when you start to doubt whether someone values you. The idea that relationships work best when they are in balance has been labelled 'social economics'. In the last chapter we saw examples of this in the concepts of status and one-downness. Unless something shifts, it is hard to sustain this sort of imbalance; the relationship will topple.

If you live with others it soon becomes apparent who is pulling their weight with the household chores. Early in his career, Rod shared a house in London with five other men. They had a monthly rota where each of them was responsible for one of the shared rooms. This meant that if you were on bathroom duty for the month, you probably wouldn't do much cleaning in there, but you certainly wouldn't touch any of the other rooms. You would dump your empty dinner plate on the draining board and sashay out of the kitchen, safe in the knowledge that it was someone else's job to clean up.

The net effect of this system was that the house was dirtier than it would otherwise have been, but the principle of reciprocity was protected.

Cognitive linguist George Lakoff has pointed out that much of the language we use is dependent on metaphor – language shapes the way we think about things and the metaphors embedded in even the simplest concepts show how we understand them. In his book *Metaphors We Live By* he gives some juicy examples. We think of ideas as food ('that's food for thought'; 'that idea is half-baked'; 'let me stew on that'). We think of love as a journey ('we've just started out together'; 'look how far we've come'; 'it's been a bumpy road'; 'we can't turn back now'). When it comes to helping, the importance of reciprocity is evident in how often we use financial metaphors. 'Can I borrow you for a moment?' 'Thanks for paying attention.' 'I owe you one.' 'Pay it forward.' 'Friends, Romans, countrymen, lend me your ears.' The notion of reciprocity is at the core of how we understand the whole concept of helping.

As I mentioned in the prologue, the idea of reciprocity has been used by biologists to explain the evolution of helping behaviours. Recent theory has suggested that prosocial behaviour evolves where strong reciprocators emerge to enforce more selfish types to toe the line. Chimpanzees demonstrate this conformity to social norms; they groom others attentively even when there is no immediate quid pro quo. The rewards come later, and not just in the form of reciprocal grooming. Members of a group who are seen to help are more likely to be accepted and protected by that group. It's the same in human society. Italian peach farmers visit each other's orchards to thin fruit on their neighbours' trees. They don't trust themselves to be brutal enough to destroy the young fruits they have nurtured. Being seen as a helpful member of the community can cement your position in that community. A few years ago, we moved from London to a small rural town. We did this partly as a result of some advice from a dear friend. She told us that her parents wished they had settled in their final destination earlier, while they were still young enough to contribute to the community.

As we have just seen, you can't talk about reciprocity without talking about money. That is how the give and take of helping is systematised in society. Money is not just integral to the language of helping transactions, much of our help is actually paid for. But that isn't the end of it: being paid isn't enough to satisfy us. We need more. At the very least, thanks. We want to be recognised for what we do. Another form of satisfaction is to know you are getting results. A personal trainer told me he avoids taking on certain clients. People come to him claiming they want to lose weight. They book weekly sessions, but some don't do any exercise between them, and ignore his dietary advice. 'I do this job to help people and I can't help them,' he said. It reminds me of the therapy-go-round.

We often do thank people in paid helping roles, and rightly too. But sometimes people use it as an excuse not to be grateful. My social psychology lecturer had a strict policy of never thanking retail staff. He said he didn't owe them anything because they were being paid to serve him. Worse than that, the fact that the helper is doing their job can be taken as an excuse for rudeness or abuse. One of the palliative care nurses I interviewed remembered consoling a colleague who had been told, 'I hope you aren't allowed to be with your husband when he dies.'

Helpers themselves can discount the value of what they do when they are paid for it. One of the people I interviewed, a learning disability nurse, had also taken up voluntary work running with blind people, a human guide dog as he put it. He wanted to do something useful because his nursing wasn't enough. 'It's my job. It doesn't count.' It's the same with self-employed helpers who baulk at charging a fair rate for their services. Some feel guilty for charging at all.

Spotlight 2.1: *Reciprocity*

Here are some questions to reflect on:

Do you expect anything in return for helping?

Have you ever felt that you shouldn't get anything in return?

Do you ever discount your helping when it is part of your job?

Have you ever felt that you are not getting enough in return?

Remember, there are no right or wrong answers. At this stage we are just building your profile as a helper. But you might need to remind yourself that it is okay to get something in return for helping. Later we will see how trying to help selflessly is not sustainable.

Altruism – The Shocking News

Now we come to the second motivation for helping. The one that doesn't hope for anything in return. Even the SAVE formula allows for the possibility that we are sometimes motivated to help when there's nothing in it for us. It does that by ingeniously including the expression $(1 + B_{self})$. The scientists who came up with the formula weren't just signing up to a blind faith in human nature, they were summarising the research.

In the prologue, I mentioned Daniel Batson and his Good Samaritan experiment. Over decades in his laboratory, Batson tried to disprove the existence of altruism. He tested every explanation he could think of and subsequent ones dreamt up by other psychologists who criticised his work. Is helping motivated by avoiding the unpleasant experience of seeing another in pain? Is it motivated by shame at being seen not to help? Is it motivated by guilt when we believe we should help? Or maybe by some sort of emotional reward, like feeling proud that we helped, as the economists have thought? Could it even be 'empathic joy', a positive feeling released when we see someone benefit from our help, but which would still ultimately offer a self-serving pay-off rather than be purely altruistic? Devising experiments to test all of these possibilities demanded all sorts of crafty setups: convincing students that they had taken a pill which would predispose them to feel empathy; tricking people into believing they could help by submitting to electric shocks on behalf of someone else. These aren't exactly typical of how we help in the real world, but they are the sort of rat maze you have to navigate if you want to test all possible motives for helping. It's a fascinating saga told in Batson's book *A Scientific Search for Altruism*. No wonder it took more than thirty years. The good news is none of them won. Altruism exists!

But what motivates altruism in the first place?

We Need to Talk About Empathy

When I ask people what motivates them to help, they typically say empathy. It seems obvious. I agree that empathy is vital, but when it comes to what motivates altruism, I believe the answer is compassion. If we gallop through the vast literature on empathy, I can point out why.

Empathy has captivated philosophers in their struggle to understand morality. It has fascinated psychologists because it is essential to social interactions. It's vital to many professions, from medical practice to talking therapies. It has been called the bedrock of morality, the glue of society, the source of everyday miracles and a universal solvent. 'Any problem immersed in empathy becomes soluble.' Everyone agrees empathy is important but it's hard to find agreement about what it is.

Cognitive Empathy – I Know How You Feel

The one thing pretty much everyone does agree on is that there are two main types of empathy. 'Cognitive empathy' is the comprehension of what someone else is feeling. We use it all of the time. We are intrigued about what is going on in other people's heads. A manager gives feedback to an employee then looks quizzically at them trying to read their reaction. Late at night, a lover frets over the minutiae of the day, and the text they just received from their new partner. Cognitive empathy is not perfect, and we seldom know how accurate we are. But in all our social interactions we invent stories to fill in the gaps in what we think others are thinking.

If we didn't have cognitive empathy much of what is done in the helping professions would not be possible. You have to understand that someone is suffering before you can alleviate that suffering. Cognitive empathy requires both inclination and skills. For example, in his training programmes for healthcare practitioners, therapist and teacher John Heron describes 'empathic divining', which he says is like picking up on something 'just below the surface', unspoken or affected. In a professional setting, the practitioner then plays that insight back to the client.

Another technique is what I call 'secondary empathy'. This involves sharing insights into what might be going on in the mind of a third party, someone in the client's life. The coach has the advantage of being outside the situation rather than lost in the emotional blur. That gives them the opportunity to make use of objective cognitive empathy, tying in their own insights with everything they have learnt from the client. One woman was upset about her volatile manager, who would put her down in team meetings. I knew how capable she was and that she had received positive feedback from her manager's boss. I wondered if her manager might be acting unfairly because he felt threatened by her. Initially my client dismissed this idea, although I could see that she would like it to be true. As time progressed and she observed his behaviour she could sense his insecurities. She began to grow in confidence. She started to focus less on what he thought of her. Ironically, she recently messaged me to say that Human Resources had approached her to apply for his job.

Cognitive empathy is a powerful tool, but like all tools, it can be used for good or bad. Marketers manipulate people's desires to sell them things they don't need or can't afford. Cult leaders exploit their insights to prey on potential followers. The impression of being fully understood is one of the attractions of joining a cult. Cognitive empathy can come without compassion. In Lionel Shriver's harrowing novel, *We Need to Talk About Kevin*, from an early age the psychopathic son discerns exactly how to hurt his mother. He refuses to potty-train, sprays paint over her meticulously decorated room, falsely sucks up to his father in front of her and so on. All calculated to destroy her nerves.

By now it should be obvious that cognitive empathy is not necessarily a precursor for helping. That is one reason I have chosen to focus on compassion instead.

Emotional Empathy – I Feel Your Pain

A friend recently came round for coffee. Three fingers of his right hand were in plastic splints, bound together with a frayed and slightly grubby bandage. A few weeks before, he had driven to watch his teenage son play football in the park. Back in the car his son was exchanging excited banter with his teammates. My friend picked up the muddy football boots forgotten on the gravel beside the car. As he handed them back, he balanced himself with his right hand on the hinged side of the door. His son took the boots and slammed the door. My friend yelled. He grabbed the handle with his left hand and prised his fingers out. They were bent like snapped twigs. They swelled and went purple. The doctor said he'd severely ruptured the ligaments. The worst part, my friend said, was that each time he went for an X-ray or to see a doctor, they wouldn't let him describe the injury. They yanked off the splints, tearing the tissue apart again.

When helpers tell me they are motivated by empathy, they mean emotional rather than cognitive empathy: their concern when someone else is suffering. Emotional empathy is the sense of experiencing someone else's feelings. There is neuroscientific evidence to show that it can be literally true when we say, 'I feel your pain.' Jean Decety, a leading cognitive neuroscientist, has shown that the same neural circuits involved in the experience of physical pain are activated by observing someone else in pain. Other brain circuitry relating to feeling threatened is activated too.

Emotional empathy can equally be an enjoyable experience. It was out of appreciating the beauty of art that Edward Titchener first coined the word empathy: a translation of *Einfühlung* – feeling into. It is what makes movies enthralling. We shudder with the same fear as the girl left alone in the horror house. We cringe in embarrassment with the geeky lover. Our hearts pound as Jason Bourne leaps across a series of rooftops. We enjoy this 'emotional contagion' safe in the knowledge that it is all make-believe. Watching sport grips spectators for the same reason.

Emotional empathy can be fun, but having fun isn't a motivator to help. While empathy allows you to feel someone's pain, it also allows you to feel their joy. That is a second reason why I have chosen to focus on compassion. In a moment we will see how compassion is a painful emotion in response to seeing suffering, and therefore a motivator to help.

The Case Against Empathy

There is evidence that cognitive and emotional empathy inhabit two separate brain systems, which are intricately woven and often active at the same time. Cognitive empathy is associated with the medial frontal cortex, which lies just behind your forehead, and emotional empathy is located in the anterior cingulate cortex, a little further back in the brain.

This idea of two separate systems has allowed Paul Bloom, a psychologist at Yale, to build a case *Against Empathy*. It might surprise you to know that anyone should disapprove of it. It might sound like he is against smiling or, as he puts it, against kittens. Let's see why. His main accusation is that empathy is a bad basis for policy decisions. Empathy can be biased. He likens it to a spotlight, shining a narrow focus; we have more empathy for those we know, or for a particular individual over a group. He draws on a well-known experiment (by none other than Daniel Batson of course) in which students were asked to make a moral choice. The students listened to a fake interview with a terminally ill girl, Sheri Summers, who was on a waiting list for a new treatment. They were asked if Sheri should be moved up the list ahead of other children who were more severely ill or had been waiting longer. Students who had their empathy system primed by being told to imagine Sheri's feelings were more likely to unfairly bump her up the list than students who were told to remain objective. The researchers concluded that empathy can lead us to make decisions that go against our own moral values. This is called the 'identifiable victim effect'. It is the reason charities don't just send you fundraising leaflets telling you how thousands are starving. To prime your empathy, they face you with the plight of a specific person staring at you with plaintive eyes.

According to Bloom, empathy is short term. He uses the example of giving to beggars. Decisions made on the basis of empathy can alleviate immediate suffering at the cost of long-term harm. Another psychologist told me about his experience of sleep-training with his son. The prevailing advice at the time was to put the child to bed and ignore any crying. He told me he sat in the kitchen, hunched over the baby monitor, listening to his son scream. It ripped out his heart. All he wanted to do was rush up the stairs and rescue his son. It was the longest thirty minutes of his life. But the parents persevered because they had been told it would be better for the child in the end. The second night was twenty minutes of torture, the third night ten. On the next, his son went to bed with the briefest whimper and slept through until morning. After that he was happy to be left in the cot and always slept peacefully. Similarly, many medical procedures depend on putting aside short-term empathy for long-term benefits. If we allowed emotional empathy to rule our decision making it would be hard to drill into a root canal or, as in the earlier example, yank off three splints to check that the fingers were setting correctly.

Bloom goes so far as to claim that 'if we want to be good and caring people, if we want to make the world a better place, then we are better off without empathy'. The professional carers I interviewed would probably be horrified by that. One palliative care nurse told me about another member of the team who 'lacked empathy and did as little as she could get away with'. Sometimes the patients would buzz for pain-killing medication during handover meetings. All the other nurses would duck out of the meetings to respond to their calls, but this nurse ignored them. One of her patients was suffering terminal agitation (the distress that some experience when they know they are close to death). He was bed-bound and desperate for a cigarette. His family asked for his bed to be pushed outside so that he could smoke to calm down. It was summer, and that was something they sometimes did. The nurse sternly refused, saying she would only give him medication. My interviewee argued with her and then went to look for a healthcare assistant to help wheel his bed outside. The man had his final cigarette and died half an hour later.

Bloom does provide a convincing argument that empathy as he has defined it (emotional empathy) is a poor basis for policy making. I accept that relying on it can be misguided, but I think he goes too far in being against empathy. Surely, most of the time, rational people don't make judgements based on emotional empathy alone. Without it we might simply not care. When I asked Melanie Wendland, global healthcare designer and co-founder of Sonder Collective, about the value of empathy, she said:

A lot of the work that is done in global health follows science and reasoning, but if you actually empathise with people, understand what they're going through and see why they're suffering it helps you to see the problems in a completely different light and then find a much better solution.

Although I agree with Melanie, the fact that empathy is not universally seen as a positive quality is the third and final reason I opted for compassion instead.

The Case for Compassion

Understanding how compassion works will allow us to understand how it can go wrong. When there is a glitch and the motivation for helping gets corrupted, this can lead to compulsive helping.

To explore this subject, let's bring the philosopher Martha Nussbaum on to the stage. Her theory of the emotions asserts that they aren't merely capricious elements of our experience – they are important value judgements. Our emotions inform the way we make decisions. Compassion informs our decision to help: 'Compassion is a painful emotion occasioned by awareness of another person's undeserved misfortune.' In her view, there are three cognitive requirements for compassion. It's as if, when we see someone who is suffering, we set a little test. We only feel compassion if they get full marks. All three requirements are important in relation to the Super-Helper Syndrome.

Here's the test:

1. Serious bad event – do you believe their suffering is serious?

2. Fault – do you believe the person deserves to suffer?

3. Eudaimonistic judgement – is this suffering against your own sense that people should flourish?

Nobody should ever attempt to paraphrase a tome of philosophy into three bullet points. Obviously, I'm painting by numbers. If you want to appreciate the original work I recommend Nussbaum's book, *Upheavals of Thought*. The first two of her requirements for compassion she takes directly from Aristotle. It's fairly straightforward on most occasions to gauge whether someone has experienced a 'serious bad event'. But there are times when you could make an incorrect judgement one way or the other. Take someone who is bitten by a mosquito. If they aren't bothered by the bite but their overly compassionate friend insists on putting them to bed and mopping their brow, then the friend has incorrectly judged this to be a serious bad event. Alternatively, a friend who doesn't see a mosquito bite as a serious bad event might simply say, 'Don't scratch it.' But if the victim has previously been hospitalised with cellulitis as a result of a mosquito bite or has a genuine reason to fear that the mosquito may carry malaria, then surely their suffering is serious, and they deserve compassion. These judgements aren't always as simple as they appear. We make them instantaneously, based on both our individual predisposition for compassion and our appraisal of the situation.

The second requirement, 'fault', also demands a judgement. The friend might be less inclined to feel compassion if they had urged the other person to put on insect repellent before going out. Judgements of fault are jostled by a crowd of factors. These relate not only to whether we consider someone to be at fault in the specific situation, but also to our overall judgement of them. If they belong to a group we feel either favourably or unfavourably towards, it can sway our view of whether they are blameworthy. If we think a particular person is nasty, we will be more inclined to believe they deserve their suffering. We each have our own threshold for the amount of fault we will tolerate in someone else while still feeling compassion towards them. Our thresholds for this differ widely – it's something I'll come back to when we look at the causes of compulsive helping. Judgements of fault are also influenced by prevailing cultural views about what people should and shouldn't do. One experiment by Jean Decety had people watch videos of AIDS sufferers in pain. The viewers reported more empathy if they thought someone had been infected as the result of a blood transfusion than if they were infected through drug abuse. Their neurophysiological responses reflected this too. When they thought the sufferer wasn't at fault, there was more activation in brain regions connected with feeling pain – they were experiencing emotional empathy.

The third requirement for compassion is what Martha Nussbaum calls the 'eudaimonistic judgement'. This is where she departs from Aristotle. He had talked about the idea of 'similar possibilities' – we feel compassion when we believe the same misfortune might happen to us. But Nussbaum says that this is insufficient for us to experience compassion. To do so, we must also feel personally affected by their suffering. As she puts it, we bring the other person into our circle of concern. One way to paraphrase her concept of the eudaimonistic judgement would be: we feel compassion when the suffering goes against our world view. Or to put it even more simply, when we care.

Spotlight 2.2: *The Compassion Test*

To feel compassion for someone we have to believe that something bad has happened to them, that it is not their fault and that we care about it. Think about your own style in relation to how you make each of these three judgements:

1. Serious bad event. How strongly do you react when someone says they are suffering? Have you felt compassion for someone but later realised they weren't really suffering? Conversely, have you ever underestimated the degree to which someone was suffering?

2. Fault. What is your threshold for believing that someone still deserves compassion even if they are at fault? Do you feel compassion for people when their suffering is clearly their own fault? Conversely, do you blame people too readily?

3. Eudaimonistic judgement. How easily are you affected by others' suffering? Do you almost always feel a personal responsibility to take action? Conversely, are you relatively unaffected by others' suffering?

Later we will see how distortions in these judgements contribute to the Super-Helper Syndrome. For now, whatever your own answers to these questions, please don't judge yourself for making the judgements!

The Compassionate Perspective

I believe compassion can be more than just a motivation for helping in specific situations. For the people I interviewed it's a perspective too. Imagine your stomach gurgles as you wait in the long queue for the conference buffet. Just as you reach the stack of white plates, someone dives in front, elbows out, brandishing their napkin-wrapped cutlery like a cattle prod. The whole queue groans. The compassionate perspective might be that perhaps they have diabetes and are about to have a hypoglycaemic attack, or to wonder if they have been told to grab a plate for the afternoon keynote speaker. Compassionate people automatically assume that the other person isn't at fault.

Or to take another example, some might think I was a bit harsh on poor old Friedrich Nietzsche in the prologue, whether or not they thought I seriously misrepresented his philosophy. If I were to have written about him from the compassionate perspective, I might have acknowledged the great pains he endured. Throughout his life he had extreme headaches and fits. He quit his professorship at Basel for health reasons. He lost his father early, was betrayed by Wagner and other friends and never found love, only rejection by Lou Salomé. He spent the last ten years of his life in dementia paralytica. It's no wonder he killed God and took a dark view of this world. But he peered through the mists to a place where man could be like a god.

Compassion as a perspective allows us to assume the good in others and approach them with tenderness. It's a predisposition or orientation – part of the helper's way of life. It expresses itself by assuming the person at the buffet is doing what they believe is the right thing. It expresses itself in helping. We could call it love. Recently I read Paul Tillich's sermon, *Love is Stronger than Death*. He wrote, not long after two world wars, that, 'We are a generation of the End and we should know that we are. Perhaps there are some who think that what has happened to them and to the whole world should now be forgotten.' That's eerily resonant for our generation too. He went on:

Often very little external help is possible. And the gratitude of those who receive help is first and always gratitude for love and only afterwards gratitude for help. Love, not help, is stronger than death. But there is no love which does not become help. Where help is given without love, there new suffering grows from the help.

If there is no love which does not become help, then we could perhaps say love, of itself, is help. It meets the definition I proposed in Chapter 1: love 'makes something easier for someone'. Love is the true heart of helping. But, when helping becomes compulsive, the suffering that Tillich talked about can be the suffering of the helper too.

Part Two

The Super-Helper Syndrome

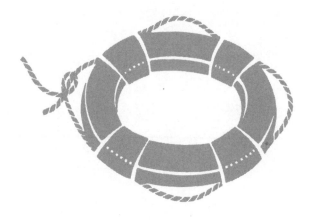

Part Two

The Super-Helper Syndrome

Chapter 3

The Unhealthy Helper

There was no shore break, just wavelets rippling onto the sand. The water looked calm and inviting. You are only just out from the shallows when you sense the current moving across your chest. Your chest? A second ago it was waist deep. You start to stride back to the beach but the sand churns under your feet. You paddle frantically and wade your longest strides but get nowhere. Panic cuts off your breath. Your legs grow feeble. Water is powering over them, through them. All that matters is to get out. Should you swim? The water is only up to your shoulders, but the sea holds you, drags you.

If you've ever been caught in a rip tide, that is what it feels like. The Super-Helper Syndrome can be like that too. It happens before you realise what's really going on. It's hard to fight it and you blame yourself. In this chapter I'll set out some of the signs so that you can stop yourself before you get out of your depth. In later chapters I'll talk about the lifelines you can use to survive.

The Super-Helper Syndrome has two main components.

A Compulsion to Help

Gambling, drugs, alcohol: compulsions can be evil. They separate families, destroy livelihoods and can even kill. What about the compulsion to help? Hang on a minute ... you would think that was a good thing. And in many ways it is – helpers have an undeniable positive impact on the people around them. But when their desire to help becomes addictive, it can actually harm the helper themselves. Unlike what happens with the other compulsions, everyone else benefits.

Spotlight 3.1: *How Much Are You Helping?*

Do you:	✓
Work in a caring profession?	
Work in a job where your primary role is helping people?	
Help people at work outside of your main role?	
Do voluntary work?	
Care for the people you live with?	
Help people in your neighbourhood?	
Support your friends?	
Look after your relatives and more distant family?	
Have responsibility for someone who is unable to look after themselves?	
Do random acts of kindness for strangers?	
Donate cash or items to charity or other causes?	

If you have a lot of ticks in the right-hand column you can probably identify with the compulsive helper. Welcome to the club. Compulsive helpers seek out opportunities to help, either directly, like offering to load a stranger's car outside the supermarket, or indirectly, like one of the nurses I spoke to who was growing her hair long to donate it to a charity that makes wigs for children undergoing cancer treatment.

I interviewed a professional photographer who had turned her art into an act of care. She photographed singles who were insecure about their dating profiles to show them relaxed and smiling. She taught partially sighted people to take pictures, and worked alongside those with mental health problems so they could learn to tell their own stories. She photographed charity events for free and founded four charitable campaigns. During lockdown she set up and ran a virtual pub quiz for her elderly neighbours. After one of her photographs of her father with dementia was shortlisted for an award, she let charities use it for free. She even found time to act as the celebrant at her friend's civil partnership. In all, she listed nineteen ways in which she helped.

Compulsive helping is not a conscious choice.

When Julia first came to see me, she was in a state of exhaustion, or to use her words, run ragged. A busy mum and wife, she worked four days a week, cared for her live-in mother and volunteered monthly as a telephone counsellor. In the evenings she was studying for a coaching diploma. In one session, she told me about a time when she was travelling home from Manchester Piccadilly station. As she dashed across the busy concourse, she spotted an elderly man glancing repeatedly from his foldout timetable to the flashing information board overhead. His suitcase had split open at his feet. Julia recalled her thoughts: 'He looks lost ... I should help him ... I'll miss my train ... I'll ask if he needs help.' She threaded him through the crowds to his platform, carrying his suitcase, and had to wait an hour for her next train.

Julia's tendency to take responsibility for the welfare of random strangers is a laudable quality. But where does it stop? What if, while boarding her later train, she had spotted another old man looking lost. Should she stop and help him too? When we discussed this, she didn't see anything unusual in her behaviour: 'Anyone would have done the same.' When I asked her what the other people in the station were actually doing, she said they were all just rushing by. The key point here is not that she shouldn't help lost strangers. The point is that she was compelled to help and was unaware of this compulsion.

You might have been thinking about yourself in relation to compulsive helping. How did you react to the examples of the photographer or Julia? Did you find yourself totting up your own list of helping behaviours and comparing your count to theirs? Did you wonder if you are doing enough? Either way, you might ask yourself if you are susceptible to a compulsion to help ...

... And Not Meeting Your Own Needs

Hands up if you meet all of your own needs all of the time. Few of us do. In my live events I ask the attendees to rate themselves on a scale of one (not at all) to ten (all the time) on how much they support others, and on how much they support themselves. I then ask them to raise their hands if they scored higher on the first question. Almost everyone puts a hand up. And those are my corporate clients, not necessarily people who would call themselves helpers. If the audience were made up entirely of those with Super-Helper Syndrome, everyone would score low for supporting themselves. Such people are so intent on meeting the needs of others they say they don't have enough time for themselves. Or they see meeting their own needs as selfish. I'll tackle these excuses when we come to the No Needs Belief in Chapter 8. For now, I want to show you the psychological and physical consequences of not meeting your own needs.

Vicki Helgeson at Carnegie Mellon University has conducted extensive research into people, predominantly women, who 'focus on others to the exclusion of the self'. Helgeson refers to this as 'unmitigated communion', building on a theory first proposed by David Bakan in the 1960s. The concept of unmitigated communion does sound closely allied to the 'not meeting your own needs' component of the Super-Helper Syndrome. Helgeson specifically refers to 'placing others' needs before one's own'. Her research has shown that those with unmitigated communion were more prone to various forms of distress, including anxiety and depression. They were also more likely to neglect their needs in several health-related behaviours such as diet, smoking, exercise and relaxation.

Spotlight 3.2: *Are You Meeting Your Needs?*

To what extent are you meeting your needs in the following areas? 1 not at all – 10 completely	1–10	Your reflections: Why don't you meet this need? Do you feel you have any control?
Health Diet, health check-ups, drinking, smoking, self-medicating		
Exercise Walking, gym, classes, sport, dance		
Psychological Rest, relaxation, meditation, talking to someone, coaching, counselling		
Home Providing and maintaining a home that feels safe, comfortable, uncluttered		
Close Relationships Maintaining healthy relationships with people who love and respect you: partner, family		
Career Working hours, levels of stress, work satisfaction, career development		
Money Income, debt, outgoings		
Fun Hobbies, holidays, adventures		

Community Friends, belonging, safety, spending time with people who support you rather than drain you		
Aspirational Personal growth, working towards being the best version of yourself		
Soul Finding meaning in life, spiritual satisfaction, faith, creativity		
We'll make extensive use of this list in Chapters 8 and 9 when we look at meeting your needs.		

Before You Get Sucked Out to Sea

We've seen that the Super-Helper Syndrome has two components: a compulsion to help and not meeting your own needs. Given that, we could express it in a little formulette:

$$CH \times NN = SHS$$

Not quite as impressive as Aleksandr Kogan's! The main point about this formula is that it doesn't imply that compulsive helping is bad per se. If you are meeting your own needs too, then that's something to celebrate. In other words, $CH \times 0 = 0$. No harm done. No Super-Helper Syndrome! The problem is, it's extremely rare to find a way to meet your own needs while compulsively helping. A second problem is that helpers don't take the risks of ignoring their own needs seriously. In the interviews I conducted there was a collective shrugging of shoulders. One mother, who had recently missed the family holiday because of her over-commitments, ruefully admitted she would only change her behaviour if her husband were to give her an ultimatum, threatening to leave. There is a sense of pride in helpers not meeting their own needs. Faced with the question in the interviews, they pulled a cheeky I-got-away-with-it smile. I could see that they wanted to please me by telling me that they knew it was important to look after their own needs. But they didn't really mean it. Compulsive helpers are determined. They take their responsibility for others seriously. They are the last ones to admit they need help. Even as the waters overwhelm them, they are waving at the beach shouting, 'No, no, you keep on playing; I'm fine.'

I feel impelled to highlight the risks. At the extreme, it can lead to what engineering professor and expert on neurocircuitry and social behaviour, Barbara Oakley, calls *Pathological Altruism*: 'the habitual, maladaptive, and/or compulsive pursuit of the welfare of others'.

One of the nurses I interviewed told me about an afternoon when she was rushing to collect her kids from school. She had been working crazy hours and was in the habit of leaving at the last minute when it was too late to wait for a bus. She flagged down a taxi in heavy traffic and got in, only to be told by the driver that it wasn't a taxi. She asked him for a lift to the school anyway. It was only when she got there and closed the car door that she realised what she had done. She was so stressed with work she couldn't see that 'it was completely mad and dangerous and stupid and mortifying'. She told me that her husband still doesn't know about this.

Organisations representing those in the caring professions are aware of the dangers. The National Association of Social Workers code of conduct urges its members 'to engage in self-care'. The American Nurses Association Code of Ethics stresses that nurses have a duty to themselves to act competently: 'Nurses should pay as much attention to taking care of themselves as they do their patients.' Sadly, few of them do. If you are experiencing Super-Helper Syndrome, it's likely to reveal itself in one or more of the following common adverse impacts.

Exhaustion – How Long Before You Drown?

I felt like everything I knew was falling apart because my mind was just so frazzled and the hours I'd been doing were ridiculous. I worked it out today actually and this year alone I've done an extra 69 working days.

Accountant, Interviewee

Exhaustion is the most obvious way that the Super-Helper Syndrome harms people. It's the most frequent reason they come to me. Initially, they try to ignore the day-to-day tiredness, what we might call chronic exhaustion. The natural tendency of helpers is to struggle on. But they soon become irritable from overworking. Some report bouts of tearfulness or forgetfulness. Long-term exhaustion can impair their judgement, for example taking on an ever-growing to-do list, or getting into a taxi that isn't a taxi. A probate lawyer explained how the busier she was, the less logical she found herself when deciding whether to take on requests for help. A strategist in heavy manufacturing told me something similar: 'The busier I get, the more difficult it is to say no.' I find this fascinating; the non-helpers I know don't seem to have the same problem.

Eventually, exhaustion gets serious. One of the teachers I interviewed was looking after her father who had terminal cancer. Her parents wouldn't accept outside care; they relied solely on her. For an extended period, she took a day off work each week, left her young family behind, and drove long distances to visit them. 'I had to push my own feelings aside and listen to my dad talk frankly about how he hoped mum would find someone else when he was gone,' she said. 'I was scared, emotional and worried. I used to cry in the car on the way home.' In the end she was put on antidepressants and signed off work by her doctor.

Helpers can also become exhausted when they don't have the resources to do their job properly, or because they face impossible demands. It can feel like the system is fighting them. I have heard countless examples of workplace exhaustion, or burnout. A special educational needs teacher was in a school that pushed its staff to their limits. Despite espousing high standards of care as a value, the school environment prevented this. They expected her to impose a rigid curriculum without allowing time for pastoral care of the children. She struggled on, working far longer than her contracted hours, frustrated that her colleagues accepted the poor standards. She ended up taking six weeks sick leave, during which time all she could do was drink white wine and watch daytime television. She felt numb and couldn't cry.

Just because someone takes a role in the caring professions doesn't mean they give up all their human rights.

Nurse, Interviewee

Another told me:

> I was the allocated nurse for six patients suffering from acute delirium
> or dementia. They'd been placed in one bay because of staff shortages.
> I didn't have anyone who was able to help with lunches. Three of the
> patients were too frail to feed themselves and I needed to go and prepare
> IV antibiotics for almost all of them. I had to choose to give people medi-
> cation rather than sitting, giving them a meal. You feel awful. You feel
> really guilty because you're not giving people the care that they funda-
> mentally need.

A well-documented form of exhaustion is 'compassion fatigue'. Charles
Figley, a leading expert in traumatology, defines this as being 'emotionally affected by the trauma of another'. Compassion fatigue drags people
away from effective caring in one of two directions. Some become toughened. They withdraw from the pain they witness. They become numb. They
lose their empathy. Others head in the opposite direction. They take on the
burden of suffering. They become unable to differentiate their own pain
from that of their clients or patients. They lose themselves. Nicki Credland,
nurse and academic, told me it is like:

> Losing your ability to show care and compassion because you're just so
> overwhelmed with the amount of support you've been giving to people –
> patients, relatives, colleagues – you've got nothing left to give to anybody
> else because you can't even manage to look after yourself.

Expressions like burnout and compassion fatigue were originally associated with professional carers. More recently, these expressions have been
widely appropriated. Everyone from fund managers to footballers talks
about burnout. Members of the public have been interviewed by journal-
ists about their compassion fatigue in relation to the Covid-19 pandemic.
These terms are being diluted. There is no comparison between the lockdown weariness we all suffered and the compassion fatigue experienced
by an ICU nurse.

Shamefully, for professional carers, the emphasis is too often on being tough in order to survive. Some job adverts for child protection staff have even used advertising slogans asking potential applicants if they are tough enough. In an attempt to mitigate this, Karen Saakvitne and Laurie Pearlman, two of the leading researchers in this area, have urged employers that they have a 'duty to warn' applicants about the potential harm of working with trauma. Similarly, the recent initiative of compassionate leadership in the health service in the UK is an attempt to reform the organisational culture to one that 'enables and sustains safe, high-quality, compassionate care'.

During my own training, one of my clinical placements was in a high-dependency unit in Liverpool. The ward, behind two securely locked doors, housed fifteen patients with severe psychiatric disorders and addictions; those who might be a risk to themselves or to the public. I only worked there for a month but faced with people who had spent whole lifetimes in psychiatric care, I struggled to close the doors on my own distress. My clinical supervisor, a psychologist in her mid-30s, who was always on the edge of tears, confided in me that she had had enough. She was going to quit the profession. She told me she could see how upsetting I found it. We both wondered whether I was cut out for this work.

Resentment – Inescapable Fetters, Grievous Bonds

Nobody wants to be an angry helper. It is the opposite of all they stand for. Acceptance and tolerance are core to their values. But one of the charity workers I spoke to put it bluntly, 'Helping too much can and does end up in resentment.' The helper doesn't want to stop. To do so would be to admit defeat. And when they feel resentful, they don't want to admit that either, not even to themselves. Resentment is a self-defeating emotion. It gnaws away at people. You might recall the gruesome punishment of Prometheus, who helped humanity by giving us fire that he stole from the gods. He was tied to a rock and had his liver pecked out each day by an eagle, only to watch it grow back each night.

Helpers have a high threshold for imbalanced relationships. They believe they should help because they can. Because they give the impression that they want nothing in return, they get nothing in return. They get taken for granted. Meanwhile, the helper is stretched like an elastic band.

> People use me as a free therapist. I get friends messaging: can I quickly just talk something over with you? But I know it will take hours. They treat me like that's my special little skill and they've got me on speed dial. I have so many friends that have dropped in, picked my brain and dropped back out again. And it's hurtful in some ways too, because then they disappear, and you don't hear about the good times. It feels like people don't understand what they're doing to you.
>
> Therapist, Interviewee

Often the people closest to the helper notice the imbalance first. This was a big theme in the interviews I conducted. One nurse told me how other parents would bring their children round to her when they injured themselves. Her husband would get angry, saying, 'For God's sake we've constantly got people at the door with their kids.' Another woman told me, 'My husband gets cross with me. I keep on and on and have quite good stamina, but he says, "Just stop! You can't do everything. Why are you taking that on and that on?"' A production manager said, 'I really hate it when people say that I help others too much. It makes it seem like I'm a walkover or mistreated.' This last example shows how resentment can take the shape of an eternal triangle between the helper, the helpee and the helper's protector.

When it dawns, they finally become resentful on their own behalf. They fantasise about standing up for themselves. They rehearse the conversation. But they keep on helping. All the while the elastic band gets tauter. When it snaps it hurts everyone; the relationship is damaged and the helper feels guilty. When this happens within families it is especially painful. This is extracted from one of the questionnaires:

> When my mum died, my dad fell apart, my sister was five months pregnant, my other sister had severe depression and my brother was a drug addict ... there was no space for my grief, lots of things to do and manage. Five years later I was getting married ... it hit me that Mum would not be there, and when I needed support, no one was there for me. They had

all moved through grief to acceptance and I struggled hugely for years ...
I now have very little contact with my Dad, his choice. I have less contact
with my sisters, their choice. I was the strong one, the capable, independent person who helped out and then got walked over.

There is something else going on in the background of many helpers' lives.
It's a generalised imbalance in all their dealings with others. Helpers give
out subtle signals that they are interested in and care about what other
people are telling them, because they do care. Others feel safe and listened
to and so they readily share their own hurts and complaints. Complete
strangers unload their stories. Helpers ignore the mild resentment this
imbalance creates. It's a low frequency tinnitus – the hum of the fridge.

I get approached by people who don't even know me. My husband says,
'You didn't even say a word and that person just told you their whole life.
How did you do that?' I'm not trying to do it! I don't want to hear the bar-
tender's life story while I'm out drinking on a Friday night [laughs]. I know
it's not happening by chance, but I don't know how to shut it down!

Psychologist, Interviewee

Exploitation – Parasitic Plants

After finishing my first degree, I jumped straight on a flight to the jungles of
Kalimantan. I took a tiny plane from Java to Pangkalan Bun, then journeyed
on for eight hours by klotok up the Sekonyer River to the orangutan research
centre at Camp Leakey. I was there to help build a proboscis monkey
research facility. I did everything from sawing and planing the wooden
planks to cutting back overgrown trails with a parang so the research assistants could follow the orangutans at night. I became intimately acquainted
with leeches.

Volunteers were told to stay in a group for our safety and on our day
off we were put in pairs. One day the girl I was paired with took herself
down to the feeding platform, leaving me resting in the sticky heat of the
wooden dorm. There was a thud. And then silence. Kusasi, the giant alpha
male orangutan, had lowered himself out of the trees to the other side of the

flimsy door. I can still see his long fingernails poking through the chicken-wire window. I have no idea how many minutes I was alone with him. It is the only time in my life I actually shouted for help. In the end, a group of the workers built up the courage to shoo him away.

When I was in Borneo, one of the local Dayak people told me about rafflesia, the corpse flower that grows on the island and gives off the stink of rotting flesh to attract carrion flies. It is the largest known flower in the world, in vibrant reds and browns. Rafflesia doesn't have any ability to photosynthesise and can't feed itself: it is entirely parasitic, living off the roots and stems of other plants.

Compulsive helpers frequently suspect they are being exploited. The sad truth is that often they are. When they don't stand up for their own needs they are easy prey. Exploiters come in many guises. Some of the parasites that feed off helpers are not consciously aware of what they are doing. Some are. And like the plants that rafflesia lives off, often helpers aren't aware that they are being exploited. Someone I know, I'll call her Suzy, is a natural helper who kept coming to mind as I was writing this book. She is a connoisseur of compassion and is always rescuing people. I have witnessed the number of people who move in and out of her life, getting what they need. Her Australian husband said that part of his job is to stand guard and watch out for all the people that latch onto her. He recounted a time when they had gone for drinks with a group. A new friend of hers, an actress, sat next to him. One of the first things this woman said was, 'I know I have so much to gain from knowing Suzy.' He reported it to his wife as soon as they got home to 'warn her off the limpet'.

Exploiters have specially evolved antennae for detecting compulsive helpers. They typically start by asking for some small piece of help or counsel. One tactic is to take on the role of victim, knowing the helper will automatically assume the role of rescuer. As the relationship develops the exploiter is thankful for the help they receive and continues to expect more.

The helper is happy too – it's their natural function. They have a compassionate perspective and try to see the good in strangers. They want to believe this new friend is not like the others. And helping makes them feel good about themselves. Over time, the exploiter probes how much they can get from this unspoken contract, accepting ever more support. Next, the reciprocity we talked about in the last chapter does a surprising and perverse trick: it stands on its head. Now, the helper owes the exploiter their help. No amount is enough. If they try to back off, everything they've done is negated. The helper becomes the one at fault.

> I was lending money to a guy for a while. Then I found out he'd been spending on my credit card. I only found out he'd maxed out on my card when I needed a new pair of shoes and it was rejected in a shop.
>
> Au pair, Interviewee

Exploiters can crop up in many parts of the helper's life. A high school friend who only ever makes contact for relationship advice. A lover who wants a servant rather than a mutually enriching partnership. A parent who inverts the responsibilities, training their child to provide for them. I interviewed a social worker, much of whose time was spent safeguarding vulnerable people from would-be exploiters. He had to arrange for the police to remove a man from a woman's flat after she had allowed him to move in. For another of his service users he was putting in place an appointee to cut off funds to a brother with a gambling addiction who had ignored previous injunctions.

Organisations, too, take advantage of people willing to donate themselves. In every voluntary association I have been part of, there was a small group downstairs pulling on the oars and a larger number sunning themselves up on deck. Demanding bosses love the compulsive helper. There were many examples of willing, conscientious and talented people not being treated fairly because exploitative managers didn't want to let go of them. In one consultancy, a senior manager was famous for the fact that nobody who worked for her ever got promoted.

Helpers fall into exploitative relationships because they are compassionate people. They remain trapped in exploitative relationships not just because they are accommodating, but because they would feel guilty abandoning someone who claims to depend on them. If you've got one rafflesia growing off you, there are likely to be more. Are you followed around by the stink of rotting flesh?

Spotlight 3.3: *The First Three Adverse Impacts*

As a result of helping other people, have you ever:

1. Experienced exhaustion?

2. Felt resentful?

3. Been exploited?

If you have experienced these three adverse impacts of the Super-Helper Syndrome, there is plenty of material to come that you can use to alleviate this or to ensure it doesn't happen again. For now, please don't take it as an opportunity to judge yourself. Remember, at this stage you are simply building up a profile of yourself as a helper.

Chapter 4

Irrational Beliefs

The rest of this book is about ways to alleviate the Super-Helper Syndrome. What I don't want to do is offer quick-fix solutions. It would be simple enough to tell people to stop compulsive helping by exhorting them to 'JUST SAY NO!' to requests for help, a suggestion that sounds like the 1980s anti-drugs campaign that led to more drug taking. It would be equally futile to tell people they should meet their own needs by soaking in a bubble bath, or other perfectly sensible small moments of self-care. Instead, we need to go deeper into the psychology of the Super-Helper Syndrome to discover its underlying causes hidden in the helper's belief system.

> There is nothing either good or bad, but thinking makes it so.
>
> Shakespeare, *Hamlet*, Act 2, Sc. 2

Beliefs drive compulsions. Many pioneers of psychology agree that our beliefs are fundamental to our emotional health and life satisfaction. Our beliefs inform what we value, how we feel and how we behave. Here, we are not talking about our personal philosophy, beliefs such as the importance of democracy or the existence of God. Of course, these do play an important role in how we understand who we are and our place in the world. But, from the perspective of psychological wellbeing what matters most are the beliefs you hold about your *self*. By this, I mean your evaluation of your personality, capabilities, appearance and so on. And crucially, your opinions about events in your life. I would like to illustrate this by using the classic A–B–C model from Cognitive Behavioural Therapy.

Activation–Belief–Consequence

Have you ever received an unexpected call and jumped to a negative conclusion the moment you saw who was calling? Say it's your boss. Your heart pounds and your stomach tightens. It's a common occurrence – for some of us it happens every time the phone rings!

We can break this down using the A–B–C model to illustrate how our beliefs affect our behaviour. The A stands for the 'activating event', in this case the phone ringing. The C is the emotional and physiological 'consequence' – your stomach tightening with dread. We are consciously aware of both the A and the C. We assume we feel anxious because of the phone call. You might berate yourself afterwards: 'Why did I get upset about such a silly thing?' What we are unaware of is that there is an intervening B, the 'belief' about the event. In the case of the phone call, the belief might be, 'I've done something wrong!' The important thing to understand is, it is the belief that causes your reaction, not the event itself. To demonstrate this, we can easily imagine an alternative response. Someone who didn't hold the negative belief might wonder, 'Why is he calling me?' Consequently, they would want to know what the caller has to say, but this thought would not trigger the negative emotional reaction. A phone call is actually a neutral event. Earlier, at the station, Julia was aware that there was an old man who looked lost (activating event) and she felt a compulsion to help (consequence), but she was unaware at the time of what was driving this compulsion (her beliefs).

Our unconscious thoughts occur astonishingly fast. When the phone rings our neurons start firing in a matter of milliseconds. By comparison, the conscious mind lumbers through its experiences, never quite catching up. There's about a half-a-second lag before the phone call clambers into consciousness. That is plenty of neural time for our belief system to go haywire. Last night I was late to our street barbecue after conducting one of the interviews for this book. Before going out to join my neighbours I went to fill a glass from the bottle in the fridge. I wondered if I should take a second glass out of the cabinet for Rod, but almost simultaneously thought, *he's out there, he'll already have a drink.* In that microsecond of indecision, I pivoted my weight four times between the fridge and the cabinet. It's the same with irrational beliefs. They happen at the speed of thought.

With the phone call, it's easy to see that the belief causes the reaction. But it isn't always so apparent. People leapfrog from A to C all the time. It happens whenever we use expressions like: 'you're embarrassing me'; 'you're upsetting me'; 'you're annoying me'. In all of these, it is our beliefs that cause the emotional reaction, not the other person's behaviour. Nobody can directly cause someone else's emotions.

Imagine you've just finished having lunch in the city. When the waiter brings the bill, your friend grabs it and says, 'I'll get this. She can't afford it.'

What would your reaction be?

Perhaps you flinch and reach for your wine glass. You stare down at the tablecloth. Your cheeks heat up. As the waiter retreats, you whisper, 'You've embarrassed me.' At this point you're aware of what your friend said and you blame her for causing your discomfiture. What you are not aware of, is that it's actually your interpretation of the event that causes your reaction. Your embarrassment is triggered by your understanding of the context – what you think of her, what you think she thinks of you, what you think the waiter thinks of you, etc. (a firework display of cognitive empathy). With a different interpretation of exactly the same event you might feel grateful, or even find it funny.

Blaming someone else for our emotions is an everyday occurrence of what psychologists call 'irrational thinking'. We all do it, all of the time. There are many types of irrational thinking; it's a topic that could fill a small library. There's one particular type I'd like to zero in on because it drives the compulsive helper.

Shoulds & Musts

Much of our thinking is in the form of instructions to ourselves. Aaron Beck, who founded Cognitive Therapy, called this the rules we live by. This type of irrational thinking is characterised by the occurrence of the words 'should' and 'must'. 'I must lose weight'; 'I should be a better parent'; 'I should go to the gym more'. The German psychoanalyst Karen Horney called this the 'tyranny of the should'. Take someone who has underlying doubts about how clever she is and feels she must prove her worth by demonstrating intelligence. She might live by the rule 'I must always get top grades'. By following this instruction, she's likely to put immense effort into studying, become a grade A student, and strive to achieve a never-ending string of academic accolades. That is how beliefs drive compulsive behaviour.

The instructions are unreasonably demanding and insidious, and in the end they are impossible to fulfil. As Aaron Beck originally put it, 'when the rules are discordant with reality or are applied excessively or arbitrarily, they are likely to produce psychological or interpersonal problems'. We end up blaming ourselves when we fail to carry out these instructions.

Self-Criticism – The Fourth Adverse Impact

We all have an inner critic, but some are more sensitive to theirs than others. It can be louder or quieter at different points in our lives. When there is more risk of failure, such as starting a new job or a new relationship, the volume of the inner critic increases. Although there are some who claim to ignore it, for many it's a background commentary droning on all the time in our heads. It's like a radio station: CRITICAL FM – broadcasting negative thoughts about you and your life 24/7!

For compulsive helpers, self-criticism operates on two levels. At the everyday level, they undervalue the adequacy of their efforts to help. They should always be doing more. Or on the rare occasion when they don't help, they find themselves ruminating on how they should have. It's the G word again. Guilt is the penal system of the inner critic. And it just keeps cropping up in relation to helpers. This is only Chapter 4, but I've already mentioned it about half a dozen times, either when talking about helpers or in quotes from their interviews. It will keep coming up. Guilt and helping go hand in hand.

> They latch on to me – I feel like I'm their therapist. They call me once a day crying down the phone for thirty minutes. And I can't say I need to go now as I'd feel too guilty. But it means I have to work late and at weekends to catch up on emails. I'm helping the client; I'm helping the company; but it's reducing my personal and emotional capacity.
>
> Estate Agent, Interviewee

As if belittling their attempts to help wasn't punishment enough, there's a second level of self-criticism. Helpers blame themselves for experiencing the other three adverse impacts of the Super-Helper Syndrome: they criticise themselves for feeling exhausted or resentful or being exploited. It's cruel and it's unjust – the inner critic is exceptional at undermining compassionate people. Self-criticism is the fourth adverse impact of the Super-Helper Syndrome.

I frequently meet people who are accomplished in their careers but don't feel it. They have distorted views of themselves, as if locked in a hall of mirrors. They are pursued by doubts that they don't know what to do. They are afraid they will offend someone or break some unknown code of conduct. This seems to me to be especially true of compulsive helpers. It's ironic, given that they are highly sensitive to the feelings of others and choose their words with extreme caution. They are the least likely to offend anyone.

For some, self-criticism is amplified beyond the background drone that undermines us all, and it can even be taken to extremes. One of the nurses I interviewed had a colleague who was good at her job and caring about the patients but haunted by self-doubt. When they did a drug round together, the self-critical nurse would triple-check everything. My interviewee had to be firm with her, saying, 'Here's the morphine. Here's the vial. Here's what we're drawing up.' The other nurse would still want to check it again. She was terrified that she would do something wrong. In the end she was signed off sick for over a year.

The first stage in taming the inner critic is to become consciously aware of it.

Spotlight 4.1: *Tuning in to CRITICAL FM*

I'd like to invite you to keep a journal of your self-critical thoughts over the next five days. This is about getting to know your inner critic in relation to all aspects of your life, not just to helping.

Capture the thoughts as soon as you can. Seeing your thoughts written down will make it easier for you to work with them.

Typical themes to listen for are criticism of your personality, capabilities, appearance and how you treat others, as well as a thousand other things. This journal will be precious source material for spotlights in later chapters.

When you complete this spotlight don't worry if your inner critic starts to sound louder, or it seems like you're having more negative thoughts. That's normal. It happens to everyone who goes through my Tame Your Inner Critic online programme. By learning to tune into it you have the potential to change your relationship with it.

Your Brain is an Assumptive Helper

Your brain is not wired to make you feel good about yourself, it is wired to protect you. That's why your negative memories and emotions stand out, to serve as warning signs for the future. You might remember that the philosopher Martha Nussbaum accounts for emotions as part of the way we think: they inform how we make decisions. Fear is a pronounced example of this. Suppose you are crossing a busy road when a motorbike speeds around the corner. Your body jumps back on to the pavement out of danger. That's the amygdala in action; the brain's early warning system. It happens before you have time to consciously think, 'Oh look there's a motorbike coming my way. It's going pretty fast. It might hit me. I should step back on to the pavement to stop myself from being killed.' Here, the amygdala is working well and probably saved your life. It automatically activated a cascade of neurological systems. Signals raced to your hypothalamus and the brain stem, leading to changes in your heart rate, blood pressure and breathing patterns. Blood was pumped to power your muscles that leapt backwards off the road.

The problem is the amygdala can be trigger-happy. The same cascade of chemical and neural responses can start firing when there is no actual danger. We sometimes perceive a threat when there isn't one, like that phone call from your boss. When you think you've done something wrong, the inner critic can set off your bodily warning systems too. You are left with the pumping heart, the sweaty palms, the butterfly stomach. It is like the smoke alarm in our kitchen. It used to go off every time we used the oven. We had to open all the windows and put on the extractor fan before we dared open the oven door. As with the phone call from your boss, it was reacting to a perceived threat rather than an actual threat.

But you can't simply disconnect the amygdala the way we ripped out the battery from the smoke alarm. That's why my approach is to tame the inner critic rather than banish or conquer it, as some people urge you to. You can't just switch off thousands of years of evolution. And you probably wouldn't want to. Neurologist Antonio Damasio studied a woman whose amygdalae were both calcified to the point of inoperability. She couldn't experience fear or reliably recognise fear in other people. Her emotions were consistently upbeat, and she was open and approachable to everyone she met. However, she was unaware of potential threats. When she was shown pictures of people who were rated as untrustworthy by those with functioning amygdalae, she indicated she would trust them. So, even if you could, it wouldn't be a good idea to disconnect the inner critic completely. The brain is wired to protect you.

We spend as much as a quarter of our lives listening to our inner voice. And using the inner voice is, in many respects, like using our 'real voice'. In his book, *How You Feel*, behavioural neuroscientist James Tresilian discusses how similar they are. Scientists have shown that efferent copies of signals for speech are produced when we listen to our inner voice, but with the output to the muscles of the mouth suppressed. When I asked him to explain this, Professor Tresilian told me:

When you speak out loud, the brain generates control signals that are transmitted to the muscles and produce audible speech. These signals are also transmitted to other brain centres where they are used to modulate our auditory experience of the words we speak and the feeling of our bodily movements that produce them. The signals that follow this route are often referred to as efferent copies of the muscle control signals. When we use the inner voice, the same brain mechanisms are at work producing control signals, but these are prevented from reaching the muscles and so there is no actual speaking. The copies, on the other hand, still work to produce a kind of auditory experience of speaking – this is the inner voice.

We can't ignore our inner voice; it's a compelling part of our experience. In order to diminish its undermining effects we need to listen to it with an unflinching ear, to understand it. That's tough work. But it's worth it. It's freeing and empowering. And it is possible.

I recommended that you start to journal it because seeing your critical thoughts written down allows you to assess them objectively: to see how cruel, untrue and unnecessary they are. Much of the thinking is on repeat. CRITICAL FM has a tediously limited playlist. Once you realise that your thoughts cause your negative emotions you can correct your thinking and thereby change the way you feel. Here are some powerful ways to achieve that.

Decentering

Decentering is a simple technique where you remove yourself from the centre of the thought. You just add the words 'I am having the thought that ...' before the self-critical thought. The intention is to remind yourself that a thought is just a thought. It's not the absolute truth and you don't have to entertain it. Decentering can diminish the emotional impact. You can use it to break free from the rinse cycle of rumination.

Spotlight 4.2: *Decentering from Your Critical Thoughts*

When you have your next self-critical thought, catch it and hold on to it; notice how it is affecting you, then add the phrase, 'I am having the thought that ...'

Here's an example: 'I shouldn't get so upset about my work.'

Decentered as: 'I am having the thought that ... I shouldn't get so upset about my work.'

This technique is powerful, not least because you can do it in a blink. You can even use it in the therapeutic moment. If you are a professional carer and you find yourself having self-doubting thoughts while you are with a client you can decenter those thoughts.

You can use decentering with other types of critical thoughts as well. The psychotherapist Carl Rogers recommended this as a way to put aside your own reactions and maintain a non-judgemental attitude. For example, a paramedic might decenter a thought like this: 'I am having the thought that he shouldn't have taken the overdose in the first place.' It's only human to have judgemental thoughts like that. Decentering exposes the thought for what it is and allows you to regain your professional perspective.

Rename Your Inner Critic

In my group programmes, I ask participants to visualise their inner critic. It's a fun way to get to know and befriend it. When you imagine the voice is no longer in your head but belongs to a persona you've created, it's easier to question what it's saying. You can visualise it as coming from something small or comical. That way, you start to disempower the inner critic.

Spotlight 4.3: *Creating a Persona for Your Inner Critic*

What does your inner critic sound like? Some say a scary witch or a cheeky chimp.

If it could take a form, what would it look like? Try drawing or crafting an image. Use whatever materials you have at hand.

Listen out for your inner critic piping up to critique your artistic efforts. Saying things like, you can't draw, it's going to look terrible, this is childish, it's a waste of time. That's a perfect opportunity to capture your inner critic at work!

Here's mine. She's called Scrutiny Fairy Nou. I'd like to thank the brilliant Coral Hawkins for drawing her. I'd like to thank Scrutiny Fairy Nou for bringing my teenage self back to follow me around!

Once you have encountered the persona of your inner critic, pay attention to what it says about you as a helper. This voice is likely to be one of the strongest drivers of your behaviour as a helper.

What Helpers Believe

Coming back to the belief system that underlies the Super-Helper Syndrome, I've identified four irrational beliefs that typically drive the compulsive helper:

1. The Good Person Belief
2. The Help Everyone Belief
3. The They-Couldn't-Survive-Without-Me Belief
4. The No Needs Belief

Each of these corrupts the motivation for helping. Rather than helping out of compassion, people slip into helping in order to satisfy rules that they've imposed upon themselves. Over the next few chapters, I'd like to walk you through these four irrational beliefs in quite a lot of detail. We will deconstruct each of them by going through a process of removing five layers. It's a bit like playing pass the parcel, where each time the music stops you take off another sheet of wrapping paper. The aim of this is to discard the irrational beliefs so that we can replace them with more constructive and sustaining ones. As well as unwrapping the beliefs, I'll provide practical guidance on how to adopt more healthy behaviours. When helpers actively support themselves as well as help others, that's the prize inside the parcel.

As with any party game, there are rules that all the players need to know. Here, I want to set up what's called an 'approach mindset'. By a mindset, psychologists mean a belief or set of beliefs that informs how we think, feel and act. There has been a great deal of attention to mindset in recent years, but like many technical terms the word can lose its currency. Sometimes people employ it loosely as shorthand for a general outlook towards life. But there is a scientific methodology behind mindset that has shown some impressive and surprising results.

The Science of Mindset

Some of the best-known experiments on the power of mindset have been carried out by Alia Crum. As well as being a Stanford psychologist, she was an internationally ranked triathlete who wondered how much the effects of exercise were determined by mindset. She studied housekeeping staff in seven US hotels because they do a great deal of exercise each day but might not perceive it as such. Hoovering typically burns 200 calories an hour and cleaning baths 240 calories. But when she asked the staff if they exercised, two-thirds of them said no. When they rated themselves on a scale of zero to ten for how much exercise they got, a third gave themselves zero: 'I get no exercise'. More irrational thinking at play.

Crum gave half the housekeepers a short briefing and put up posters in their workplaces with messages like 'YOUR WORK IS GOOD EXERCISE!' and 'CONGRATULATIONS ON LEADING AN ACTIVE LIFESTYLE!' She told the staff that they were already meeting the surgeon general's recommendations for daily exercise, and she listed eleven health benefits they should expect to see from their work. The other half of the staff in the control group were just given advice that exercise is important.

Crum took measures including blood pressure, weight and levels of job satisfaction. Four weeks later, the housekeepers who had been told their work constituted exercise had lost an average of ten points on their systolic blood pressure and 2lb of weight. Their levels of job satisfaction also improved. Those who had simply been told that exercise is important didn't show any significant gains. The shift in mindset from 'work is just work', to 'work is exercise' appeared to deliver health benefits with only a fifteen-minute intervention.

You might be thinking, as I did when I first read about this, that's amazing but maybe there is something else that could explain the results. Perhaps the housekeepers started putting in more elbow juice (although they claimed that they didn't). Alia Crum had those concerns too. So, she did another experiment.

In the Mind over Milkshakes study, she invited people into the laboratory at the Yale School of Medicine to taste two milkshakes: the Sensi-Shake and the Indulgence Shake. The participants were also asked to evaluate the milkshake labels. The Sensi-Shake label offered 'Guilt Free Satisfaction' and listed zero fat, zero added sugar and only 140 calories. The Indulgence Shake was labelled as 'Decadence you Deserve', a rich creamy blend of premium ingredients with 30g fat, 56g sugar and a whopping 620 calories. While the volunteers drank the milkshakes, they were hooked up to equipment that drew intravenous blood samples. The researchers monitored levels of ghrelin, the hunger hormone. Ghrelin is secreted in the gut to tell us we are hungry. When we eat, ghrelin levels go down and we feel full. As people drank the Indulgence Shake their ghrelin levels dropped three times as much as when they drank the Sensi-Shake. That is in line with what a nutritionist would expect from the quantity of fat and calories consumed. But there was a twist: the Sensi-Shake and the Indulgence Shake were actually the same drink, containing 380 calories. The only difference was the labelling. What the milkshake drinkers believed to be going on, directly affected the behaviour of their intestinal tracts. It was the same as with the blood pressure of the housekeepers. The mindset of the volunteers determined how their bodies reacted.

Researchers have tapped the power of mindset in all sorts of applications: from influencing adolescents to eat more healthily to finding more security in romantic relationships. One of the startling things about mindset interventions is that they work even when you know what is happening. Unlike the milkshake experiment, most of them don't rely on duping anyone. If you want to look up more of them, there's a collection in the *Handbook of Wise Interventions* edited by Gregory Walton and Alia Crum. For compulsive helpers, mindset science is a lifebuoy that offers the possibility of rescuing them from irrational beliefs.

Mindset Warm-Up

In a moment I'll introduce you to the method for deconstructing the four irrational beliefs. But first, this is where I'd like to invite you to set up an approach mindset. It's like doing a warm-up routine before a workout in the gym.

You've been carrying your beliefs around all your life. Deconstructing them can be awkward or make you feel vulnerable. The natural response is to resist or deny uncomfortable realities. This has been called the avoidance mindset. Neuroscientists have used imaging techniques to show that this is associated with a different area of the brain from what they call the approach mindset. When people experience anger, anxiety or similar emotions, the avoidance system activates in the right prefrontal cortex. When people experience curiosity, enthusiasm or the like, the left prefrontal cortex activates – the approach system. Perhaps that's why it's difficult for us to feel anxious and curious at the same time.

Spotlight 4.4: *Setting up the Approach Mindset*

The approach mindset is the mode of thinking I'm inviting you to adopt as you begin to unwrap any irrational beliefs. Now would be a good time to stop and reflect on your reactions so far. How have you felt about the examples you have read? Have you felt an association with the people I've interviewed, or even a desire to protect them? If you suspect you might be a compulsive helper, do you have any resistance to exploring this further?

The spotlights to come will invite you to examine your beliefs, or experiment with new ways of being. If you're ready to get stuck in, great!

But if something is holding you back, either now or as you start deconstructing the beliefs, that is the time to acknowledge the resistance. Please know that it's a normal part of the journey. Welcome the discomfort and notice how it feels. There's no right or wrong; there's just your experience.

Remember that by activating curiosity you can dampen any anxiety. Come to the spotlights in a playful, have-a-go way.

Deconstructing Irrational Beliefs

You take the first layer of wrapping paper off the parcel by acknowledging that you HOLD the belief. There's no chance of refuting or replacing a belief if you are not even aware of it. I've found that people acknowledge some of the four beliefs more readily than others. So, when the belief is harder to acknowledge I've indicated this with an avoidance mindset red flag.

You remove the second layer of wrapping to EXPOSE the belief as irrational. Again, that is easier for some of the beliefs than others. I've red-flagged that too. For some of them, you may accept intellectually that the belief is irrational, but still not be willing to let go of it. That's why we also have to EXPOSE the belief as harmful. That's the third layer of wrapping on the parcel. Here we are thinking about the harmful effects associated directly with holding the particular belief. Those come in addition to the adverse impacts of the Super-Helper Syndrome. In fact, they exacerbate those adverse impacts, especially self-criticism. The inner critic is a big fan of irrational beliefs. Because they are unreasonably demanding and insidious there's ample opportunity for the inner critic to triumphantly point out when you fail to live up to them.

> There is power and joy in letting go.
>
> Stephen Post, 'The Way of Forgiveness'

The fourth layer is to LET GO of the belief. Letting go can be a powerful or melancholy experience even when the change itself is something we've chosen. Think about a time when you moved home. You were looking forward to the new house: it had more space; it was in a better part of town. But as you wandered around the bare rooms of your old home, you saw the discolouration of the paintwork outlining where your pictures used to hang – ghost-frames on the wall. You recalled all the good and all the bad times you had there.

Organisational consultant William Bridges drew attention to this with his transitions model. For change to work out well it requires three stages: endings, a transition phase and new beginnings. It's easy to overlook the endings stage, or to rush through it. But this can sabotage the positive results we hope to gain. Sometimes we need to pause and mark the ending or make a ritual of it, like when we gathered in the playground on Rod's son's last day to watch the children release balloons in the indigo of the school colours.

When letting go of irrational beliefs it may be necessary to forgive yourself – for having held the belief for so long, or for the impact it's had on your life. Take time to reassure yourself that it's safe to let go of it; your world won't shatter. For some of the beliefs, to be truly free of them, you may need to forgive other people too. Perhaps those who instilled the belief in you, or those who have used the belief to exploit you. Forgiving others doesn't mean you accept that what they did was right, or that it didn't harm you. Forgiveness allows you to release any anger or resentment you may still be holding on to.

Once the belief has been completely unwrapped we can PUT something in its place. For each of the four you'll find I've suggested an alternative, more healthy belief. I've also recommended new behaviours that are aligned with and designed to reinforce the new beliefs. That's the really healing part.

Letting go –
Montpelier Primary
School, 2007.

Chapter 5

The Good Person Belief

From what I've observed, the most common belief that compulsive helpers hold is about what it means to be 'good'. For them, it means to be 'helpful'. This might sound obvious to you. But let's remember, not everyone equates being good primarily with helping. A painter, shut away in a studio, might think of themselves as good because they bring beauty into the world. A police officer believes being good is upholding the law. A fervent environmentalist might define it as adopting a plastic-free lifestyle and joining protest marches against climate change. When they come face to face across a barricade in Trafalgar Square, the environmentalist and the police officer would both justify their own actions as good.

> I've always thought it's my duty to help others.
> Everyone should do it, but not everybody does.
> > Healthcare Strategist, Questionnaire Respondent

Our perspectives on what constitutes being good are multifarious. While for some, helping others might not be uppermost in their personal definition, we would all agree helping is a good thing to do. This idea becomes problematic when it turns judgemental – you're *only* a good person if you help other people. This is one of the traps helpers fall into. They apply the judgemental instruction to themselves: 'I *must* help others to prove I'm a good person.' I call this the Good Person Belief.

Childhood Messages

Her mother heard the noise,
And she thought it was the boys
A-playing at a combat in the attic;
But when she climbed the stair,
And found Jemima there,
She took and she did spank her most emphatic.

Henry Longfellow, 'There Was a Little Girl'

The Good Person Belief develops from a young age – when a child, especially if she's a girl, is socialised to believe she is only going to get approval if she's helpful. Picture a little girl who finds one of her classmates crying in the playground with a grazed knee. She takes her to the school nurse who tells her she's a really good girl. After dinner, as she dashes off to play with her brothers, her mother calls her back, 'Be a good girl and help me clear the plates.' Later, she's praised for reading her younger sister a story at bedtime. Next morning, she is told off because she hasn't made a birthday card for grandma. You get the picture!

> I got noticed when I was a good girl. Praise made me feel like I was good enough. I can see where my people-pleasing comes from. Thirty-seven years of autopilot is hard to break.
>
> Support Worker, Questionnaire Respondent

It's hardly surprising when our little girl begins to internalise her parents' and teachers' messages. Those messages are underpinned by societal norms which pretty much always subscribe to what's known as the Golden Rule: you should treat others the way you would like to be treated. Most religions stress the importance of living a 'good' life in order to gain rewards at a later date. For them, too, good is associated with how you treat other people. Both old and new testaments of the Bible tell us to 'love thy neighbour as thyself'. For Christians, when that verse was quoted back to Jesus, he said, 'DO THIS AND YOU WILL LIVE.' It's in scary capital letters in my copy of the Bible. Similarly, in the law of karma in Buddhism and Hinduism, your actions in this life determine your fate in your future existence. One exhortation to goodness in the Upanishads reads, 'This same thing does the divine voice hear, thunder, repeat: *Da! Da! Da!* that is, restrain yourselves, give, be compassionate.' People with the Good Person Belief are devout adherents of the Golden Rule.

Ervin Staub and his family fled from the Nazis when he was 6. He and his sister were saved by Maria Gogan, a woman who had previously worked for his family and took them into hiding. She was the inspiration for Staub's subsequent life. As a professor at leading American universities, he went on to study the subject of good and evil. Most recently, aged 82, his training programmes to discourage excessive use of force have been adopted by more than thirty police departments across the US, in the wake of the killing of George Floyd. In *The Roots of Goodness and Resistance to Evil*, Ervin Staub says: 'What happened to me as a child in Hungary has left me with a lifelong mission to get people to respond to those who need help.'

In his academic work too, Staub asserts that the role of the helper is reinforced in early life. He quotes evidence that children who are labelled as cooperative start to think of themselves as helpful, caring and kind. When a child learns that it can console another child or a distressed puppy, it becomes aware of its own power to do good. According to Staub, when we successfully help someone, 'we see our power to protect'. This increases our sense of effectiveness as people and our sense of responsibility to help. We then try to live up to this image of ourselves.

Our little girl sees herself as a good person when she helps; she criticises herself when she doesn't. She feeds off the praise and rewards. She lives in fear of these being taken away. She's on her way to becoming a compulsive helper. Over time, the Good Person Belief becomes part of her operating system. Helping becomes habitual. When I studied forensic psychology, we learnt about the concept of the criminal career. A young offender starts off by committing minor misdemeanours like nicking sweets from the shop. They broaden their skill set to commit more ambitious crimes as they move up the ladder. I'm struck now by how similar it is with the Super-Helper Syndrome – as a child you're on the first rung of the helping career ladder!

Once the irrational belief takes hold, no amount of helping or 'good behaviour' can dislodge it. It's the same for the grade A student who believes she isn't clever enough. Her string of academic accolades doesn't satisfy her. Flying home from Stockholm with the Nobel Prize for Physics tucked in her overnight bag, she still doesn't feel clever enough. As she removes the plastic lid from her food tray, in her head she is still working her way down the list of other candidates who are far cleverer than her and deserve this more. If that sounds ridiculous, remember irrational beliefs are often impossibly demanding as well as unconscious. We notice other people's but we are blind to our own.

Whether the self-instruction is 'I must study hard' or 'I must help people', the compulsive behaviour doesn't deactivate the underlying belief. The bad news is nothing does. It's like when you take a driving test. The examiner sits beside you watching your every move. They can even see if you check the rear-view mirror. You are constantly being assessed. If you hold the Good Person Belief, the test never ends. No matter how much you help others, you criticise yourself. Unless you can find a way to correct your thinking.

Deconstructing the Good Person Belief

Acknowledge You HOLD the Belief

Do you believe, 'I must help others to prove I'm a good person'?

At first glance it might seem unlikely, and the word 'must' sounds like an exaggeration. It isn't something you would ever say to yourself. But again, it is an unconscious belief. If you're unsure whether you hold the belief, ask yourself these questions:

Do you equate being good with helping?

Do you feel guilty when you don't help?

Were you heavily socialised to help as a child?

If I told you that you don't need to help people, does that terrify you?

If you answered yes to one or more of these questions, it's a clue that you subscribe to this belief. Notice the G word again. Helper's guilt is a strong indicator of the Good Person Belief. If you're thinking: 'But I am a good person. It's good to be helpful. If I can help, I should,' then I bet you hold the Good Person Belief. It's not that difficult to acknowledge. The challenging part comes next ...

EXPOSE *the Belief as Irrational (Avoidance Mindset Red Flag)*

I've found that with people who hold this belief, demonstrating that it is irrational can be a bit of a tussle. They hold on to it as a matter of principle. They insist that good people do help others, and they want to be good people. The belief is part of their identity. It seems self-evident, incontrovertible, blinding. As one woman put it to me, 'If I'm not good, what am I?'

So, with a certain amount of trepidation, let's have a go. Let's look at why it's irrational. First, as we've seen, there are many ways to define what we mean by good. This fact alone is why if you don't hold the Good Person Belief then you can immediately see that it's illogical. Just as we can all see that the grade A student's belief was ridiculous. But that argument doesn't wash for people who do hold this belief. The idea that something else means good is anathema to them. Good means helping. Full stop. But compulsive helpers are inconsistent in their application of this. They don't hold other people to the same rule they live by. They don't expect anyone else to help other people to prove *they* are good. They don't, for example, believe that the people they help or care for are bad because those people need help and so are unable to offer it.

Another reason the belief is illogical is because it implies that if you stop helping you stop being good. But Julia wouldn't stop being a good person if she rushed home without assisting the elderly gentleman at the station. In any case, it's impossible to always be helping. Would Julia stop being a good person if she fell ill? Or, inevitably, when she gets too old to help others?

EXPOSE *the Belief as Harmful*

If you hold the Good Person Belief, sooner or later you have to recognise that your compulsive helping is motivated by attempts to win approval. You are trying to convince others, and ultimately yourself, that you're a good person. Fundamentally, you are trying to earn love. But it's a game you'll never win. No amount of external approval will ever satisfy the belief. And as we all know, love can't be earned, even if that's what we were taught as children. The tragedy is, when your self-worth is conditional, you are in an abusive relationship with yourself. Too often, clients come to me because, in their desperate attempts to win approval, they have lost sight of who they are and what they want from life.

LET GO of the Belief

It can be deflating when you see the Good Person Belief for what it is. It's painful to have it pointed out that, through no fault of your own, your primary driver for helping people has been to gain love. You might want to close this book and never pick it up again. I don't blame you; it's natural to feel some resistance. You might find yourself clinging to the belief: 'But a good person does help people.' Or you might be calling yourself selfish: 'I've only been helping people to prove I'm a good person.' Or feeling sad: 'My sense of self-worth is so fragile.' You might need to forgive yourself for any of those feelings before letting go of the belief. You might also need to forgive your parents or anyone else who taught you to believe that you're only good when you help others.

PUT Something in its Place

Since you've read this far, then you might be interested in adopting an alternative belief: 'My self-worth is not dependent on helping others.' I hope you can see that this belief does not, for one second, suggest that you stop helping other people. It just decouples it from your self-worth. I've also got rid of the tyrannical 'must'. There's no internal command to do anything. This alternative belief gives you the freedom to choose what you want to do.

If you resolve to let go of this belief and sign up to the idea that your self-worth is not dependent on helping others, you might start wondering what your self-worth can depend on? That's the fun part.

You're Already Good Enough

In the prologue we saw that the prevailing image of human nature from philosophy and science has often been pessimistic. And when we focus the lens on individual people, they judge themselves negatively too. Now we're going to turn up the magnification to consider a specific human being: you. Are you essentially a good or a bad person? If you were to rate yourself over-all, right now, on a scale of minus ten (extremely bad) to plus ten (extremely good), what score would you give yourself?

Ideally your answer to that was:

> That's a stupid question. How could I possibly rate myself? Some of the things I do are good and some are not so good. I have my positive attrib-utes and I have my flaws. I sometimes live up to my personal standards of behaviour. And sometimes I let myself down. But I am not the sum total of my behaviours, abilities, and personality traits. It would be idiotic for me to have any sort of overall assessment of myself.

Sadly, it is rare for anyone to come up with that answer. We find it all too easy to give ourselves an overall rating. Even more sadly, most of us don't rate ourselves highly. Our inner critic makes sure of this. We underplay our positive qualities. We pitch into ourselves for the things we haven't done. This is especially true of compulsive helpers. When I described the Good Person Belief to my interviewees, several of them who had been relaxed, talkative and expressive went quiet. They sat back in their chair. They folded their arms. Then they looked away, avoiding eye contact with the camera. I could see they were thinking hard. Then they would reluctantly acknowledge that it resonated.

In real life, of course, we don't use a minus ten to plus ten scale to give ourselves an overall rating. We rate ourselves when we think, 'I am not good enough'; 'I should be a better person'; 'I am flawed'; 'I am a failure'; 'I am a pushover'; 'I'm not loveable'. Those aren't necessarily conscious thoughts, but you notice the consequences – you feel bad about yourself. If you are going to cancel your subscription to the Good Person Belief and find some self-worth that is unrelated to helping, I need to convince you either to stop rating yourself altogether or at least to start consistently rating yourself more positively. I could simply give you an affirmation saying, 'I am strong and brilliant', and tell you to repeat it to yourself five times a day while puffing yourself up in front of the mirror. And of course, you could try that. But that's not how a mindset shift works. Instead, I want to show you some rational arguments from some of the deepest thinkers.

Don't Read the Label

Why is asking you to rate yourself a stupid question? Firstly, it involves labelling yourself: 'I'm good', 'I'm bad', etc. Several philosophers have pointed out that this is nonsense. Alfred Korzybski, who founded the field of general semantics, argued it's an incorrect use of language to use a label like 'Jess is unkind'. It's referring to an abstract concept. Korzybski would say two abstractions: 'Jess' and 'unkind'. The organism known as 'Jess' cannot be fully known; the word means different things to different people at different times. Even I cannot claim to know everything about the person I call 'Jess'. Few of the cells in my body are the same as when I was a child. The me I know today is not the me I knew then. And we certainly have no shared understanding of what it means to be 'unkind'. The meaning of any word is open to infinite interpretations. Words like unkind are what Korzybski called 'high order abstractions'. He argued that there are structural semantic problems when we say something *is* something. It's especially problematic when we use 'is' about a person. His theory is complex and fascinating, even Korzybski himself joked that the original version of his magnum opus, *Science and Sanity*, needed its strong sewn-cloth binding to protect it when exasperated readers flung it from high windows. But it's easy to see how labels such as 'Jess is unkind' are harmful. They are another example of irrational beliefs. Wouldn't it be better to just stop labelling yourself?

A hugely influential American psychiatrist, David Burns, has provided a whole host of techniques to 'untwist your thinking'. He too tackles the sort of labelling that Korzybski objects to. We can follow the course of arguments prescribed by Dr Burns if we take an example. Say you were to label yourself 'selfish'. When you try to define what you mean by 'selfish', you will see that this word too is open to unlimited interpretations. Dodging that one, perhaps your definition of selfish is 'someone who does selfish things'. But under that definition we're all selfish because we all do selfish things from time to time. Unless you concede that all human beings are selfish your definition can't be valid. And if they are all selfish then your being so isn't so bad, is it? You're just saying you're the same as everyone else. Or, you might define a selfish person as someone who does selfish things more than other people. But what does that mean? How many others? Which people? How often? You might say a selfish person does selfish things more often than half the human race. But wait a minute – you are arbitrarily allocating a cut-off point that condemns half the human race to being selfish. And there's no way to know who makes the grade. You may as well walk through town randomly pointing at passers-by: selfish person, unselfish person, unself-ish person, selfish person. And so on. Since there really is no such thing as 'a selfish person', then you can't possibly be one. Once again: wouldn't it be better to just stop labelling yourself? And wouldn't that be liberating!

How to be Good

Going back to our overall topic of what it means to be a good person, the man to consult is Robert Hartman. He spent his whole life trying to answer that question. Hartman was a pioneer in the study of axiology (from the Greek *axios*, meaning value) and, in particular, human value. He was shaped by his own encounters with fascism. When he was 19 and back in his native Germany after studying in Paris and London, he started to write articles against Hitler. When he stood up and denounced the Nazis at one of their public meetings he was hurled out through an open window. After Hitler became Chancellor of Germany, they came looking for Hartman. He was saved because he was in hospital, recovering from a mental health break-down after working non-stop for seven days and nights on a paper called *The State and the Political Parties* that condemned the Nazis. He had planned to present the paper at a faculty seminar at Berlin University where he worked, but after much deliberating about his own future, and guilt about those he would leave behind, in 1933 he decided to flee Germany. He selected a forged passport from a pile on the table at a meeting of social democrats, and later changed his name to become Robert S. Hartman. He also committed the remainder of his career to finding out why good people never have as much power as bad ones.

His grand ambition was not simply to understand what constitutes 'good', but to turn that understanding into a science that would elevate the so-called social sciences to exact sciences. Whether he achieved that, I don't know. Despite his detailed mathematical and logical analysis, drawing on his background in engineering, many of his ideas are gathering dust. Paul Weiss, the Sterling professor of philosophy at Yale, wrote that although the majority of US philosophers ignored Hartman, some said his work might outlast his lifetime. Well, I guess that must be true as he died in 1973. His core axiom, his discovery of what it means to be good, is strongly appealing. It didn't come easily to him and that's not surprising; it was a question that had long perplexed philosophers. As Plato said, in *The Republic*, 'I can't tell you what goodness is, I can only tell you what it is like. It is like the sun that radiates everything, that warms everything, that makes everything fertile and brings forth everything.'

Hartman wasn't satisfied with Plato's poetic answer. After suffering hardship as a refugee he finally shook off the Nazis who had trailed him across Europe. He ended up teaching philosophy in Mexico and the US. He read all the thinkers who had wrestled with the question of what 'good' means, and he collected thousands of examples of its use from dictionaries and wherever he found the word in print. It was a long endeavour, but to know what good meant seemed to him an essential question. About that time the atomic bombs were dropped on Japan.

Then one Christmas Eve, he got it, like an extra present under the tree. He realised that *good* wasn't a property of an object but is the result of the object possessing the necessary properties of the class of things it belongs to. He wrote, 'A thing is good when it has all the properties it is supposed to have.' Hartman's axiom is easy to apply when thinking about simple objects. Take an apple. Is it a good apple? We have a pretty clear idea about the properties an apple should have. Crunchy, juicy sweetness, for example. It should be shaped like a planet. It should be green or red, never orange. Integral with a shiny clear surface. No bruises, holes or maggots please. If it has all that, let's call it a good apple. But what about you? What about moral goodness? Hartman said that to be a good you is to be honestly, sincerely and authentically true to yourself. Or as he put it, your 'Self'. But unlike the apple, it is not obvious what properties a Self should have in order to be good. What makes a good Self? Hartman's answer is that only you can define your Self:

> The more I am aware of my Self, the more, and the more clearly, I define and fulfil my Self, the more I am a morally good person, a good 'I'. I am morally good if I am as I am.
>
> Robert S. Hartman, *Freedom to Live*

Being True to Your Self

That answer is both refreshingly simple – all I have to do is be me – and also brain-bendingly difficult. What is my Self? As we saw just now, it is impossible to define ourselves completely. We are many things. Think of all the roles you fulfil. And you change, minute by minute and throughout your life. We all have infinite possibilities for our Selves. But few of us have a strong sense of our true Self. We live by the rules we've been taught. We are governed by what society expects of us. Beyond listing the helping roles they fulfil, many helpers have little sense of their true Self. That's not surprising – if you were brought up to pay attention only to the needs of others, there's no room to find out who you are, what matters to you and what you want from life.

The quest to find your true Self is an adventure. It can bring a sense of possibility, freedom and joy as you learn to live more authentically as you, rather than as a reflection of what others have wanted you to be. Especially if you were constrained during your childhood. This has been one of the major themes of my life, so I'd like to share some of that journey with you.

As a child, I was told to use no more than two sheets of toilet paper when I went to the loo. My mother monitored how much I used. If I didn't replace the empty toilet roll when it ran out, she would shout at me. She didn't let me play with any toys that were given to me. They were kept in their boxes in case she wanted to sell them. Once, when I was at primary school, my mother let me go on a Christian camp. She bought me white dungarees and a neon orange jumper, which I carefully packed. I was thrilled to have new clothes because she mostly bought stuff at jumble sales when we toured the church halls of south-east London. As soon as I got to the camp, I unzipped my suitcase. The dungarees and jumper were gone. She'd also taken out some of the other clothes I'd packed. By the age of 10 it was my job to cook and clean. I was old enough to do my own laundry. When she came back from work I had to listen for her key in the door. Then I'd rush to put the kettle on. It had to be boiling by the time she came into the kitchen. In a controlled environment like that I learnt to be an attentive listener. I learned to be quiet. I learnt to anticipate her needs. But I didn't develop a strong sense of who I am, of my Self. Not until later.

Few of us know who we truly are, especially when we are growing up. For me one of the first glimpses came when I was 13. I'd been having chronic headaches and had been taken for various tests that showed nothing was wrong. A neurologist who was due to give me the results of a CT scan asked my mother to step outside the room for a moment. When we were alone, he asked me what was really the matter. 'Just give me someone to talk to,' I said. That's how I ended up seeing a psychiatrist, and that's when I discovered what I wanted to be. I also vowed that I would try not to be anything like either of my parents. At that time, I had a clear vision that one day I would run some sort of residential family wellbeing centre. That part hasn't happened yet, but it was a first glimpse of who I could become. We all have these stories. They are pivotal points in our lives. If we trust them, follow them and cultivate them we can grow closer to our true Self.

Hartman suggests that you need to go through four stages to develop your Self:

1. Know yourself – really spend time and effort to understand what kind of person you are quintessentially.
2. Choose yourself – accept who you are and make the best of the resources within you. Hartman stresses that those resources are limitless.

3. Create yourself – become the very best version of you. Move constantly in the direction of authenticity.
4. Give yourself – forget all limitations and be generous in giving to your fellow humans.

One of the things I love about this is that when you get to the final stage, it's about helping others. As I've said before, I'm not trying to stop anyone from helping. The sad thing is that compulsive helpers jump straight to giving themselves before they have worked out who they really are and what they really want and without the power and inner resources they need.

When Your Self-Worth is Conditional

One of the leading thinkers on the subject of irrational beliefs was the psychologist Albert Ellis, founder of Rational Emotive Behaviour Therapy (REBT). I've drawn on some of the techniques from REBT in order to suggest ways that you can build the sense that you are already good enough. Ellis blossomed out of existential philosophy and was influenced by Hartman, Korzybski and Tillich. He wrote more than fifty books about his principles and therapeutic approach. REBT has been applied in clinical and organisational psychology, psychotherapy and coaching settings. As with the other cognitive therapies, REBT is based on the premise that a person's cognition, feelings and behaviour are all closely interlinked and by correcting the thinking, it is possible to relieve psychological problems. That is exactly the approach we are taking to deconstruct the irrational beliefs.

According to REBT, any form of conditional self-worth is harmful. Conditional self-worth is where we stack up our achievements to try to build a positive view of ourselves. Imagine Gonzales trains for his first marathon. He throws his arms in the air as he crosses the finishing line in under four hours (the runner's high). If his self-worth is conditional on his successes, his elation won't last. It's the same if you rely on helping others to feel good about yourself. You feel temporarily pumped up, but conditional self-worth goes down faster than a faulty air bed. And it's just as uncomfortable when you wake up flat on the floor. It begins to deflate because we accommodate our successes. When Gonzales runs his next race in the same time, he doesn't get the same boost. Only running even faster can maintain his self-worth. If he runs slower he feels wretched. Conditional self-worth also gives rise to negative social comparison. However fast Gonzales runs, there's always a host of people in front of him. Conditional self-worth is insatiable.

> If I find out that someone has been struggling, and I didn't know, and therefore didn't help them, then I feel terrible about myself.
>
> Artist, Questionnaire Respondent

Is Unconditional Self-Acceptance Possible?

I hope it is plain we need something to replace conditional self-worth. The strict alternative, one of the pillars of REBT, is unconditional self-acceptance. The idea is to separate your sense of self-worth from your behaviour. REBT suggests that we should simply accept ourselves regardless of our abilities, personality traits, life experiences, successes and failures. It suggests we should refuse to rate ourselves at all.

For me, unconditional self-acceptance is like a beautiful mirage in the desert: every time I get close to it, it dissolves. There's a sense of falseness too, as if I'm trying to kid myself that it has worked: that I've completely quit rating myself. I buy the intellectual arguments of course, otherwise I wouldn't have spent pages above telling you about them. But when I do let go of any overall judgements about myself, it leaves a vacuum: one that fills all too soon with new self-judgements. At first, I congratulate myself for how well I'm holding a space of total non-judgement. Then I berate myself for that thought. Oh, the irony! If you can take on unconditional self-acceptance, I envy you. But even by saying that, I let slip my dirty habit of comparing myself unfavourably with people I haven't even met yet. I'm not convinced that I could ever authentically sustain a completely non-judgemental view of myself. And to be fair to REBT, Ellis himself admitted that adopting unconditional self-acceptance takes persistence and a great deal of willpower, with frequent sidetracking and backsliding. For myself, I'd rather aim for something that is equally beneficial but doesn't involve pushing a boulder up a mountain.

Claiming Unconditional Self-Worth

A less onerous solution, and one that I do recommend, is to claim unconditional self-*worth*. By that I mean you choose to value yourself highly, with no small-print conditions. You take a positive view of yourself for no other reason than that's what you've decided to do. You rate yourself highly, regardless of your behaviours, abilities and personality traits. If that sounds difficult, that's because it is. But remember that you already do this when it's not about yourself. You give unconditional approval to people, and even pets, that you love. When your eight-month-old spaniel craps on the carpet, you love them nonetheless.

While I acknowledge that an unconditionally positive self-rating is arbitrary and perhaps can't be logically justified, it's a lot kinder than the common default setting. Rating yourself negatively is equally arbitrary and no more logical. Unconditional self-worth is a rebuttal of the self-denigration that most of us adopt without question.

Making use of the −10 to +10 rating scale again, how high do you dare to go? What would it be like if you gave yourself a +10? If you woke up tomorrow at +10, what would you do differently? What's the highest score you could maintain? Here's a spotlight to try if you want to give unconditional self-worth a go. There are plenty more spotlights later in this chapter to support and encourage you.

Spotlight 5.1: *The Super-Fan Mindset*

If you want to adopt unconditional self-worth it can help to think about the mindset of a dedicated sports fan. They might have chosen the team they support arbitrarily, but once they make that affiliation they stick with it through thick and thin. Whether the team is promoted or relegated they keep cheering. Individual players and managers come and go but the fan still loves the club. If the manager or the players behave badly, they still love the club. They wear the colours and feel proud. If anyone else criticises their team, they jump to its defence.

How would it be if you applied that mindset to yourself?

In contrast to unconditional self-acceptance, you can build up unconditional self-worth over time. You might not be comfortable giving yourself a +10 today but you can claim more self-worth than you had yesterday. There is always room for more. With self-worth you can have moments when it's really high without the immediate slap on the wrist when you realise you've started to judge yourself. You're allowed to judge yourself, but only positively.

When given the option to adopt unconditional self-worth, one question my clients raise is whether rating themselves highly will make them arrogant. That's understandable, but it does show how hooked they are on berating themselves. Anyone struggling with the Super-Helper Syndrome is so far from arrogant, this leaves me almost speechless. It's the worry we have whenever we are trying to correct something; that we'll overcorrect – that we'll go too high, too far, too soon. It appears so often I call it Full Moon Phobia. We'll see it come around again. The very fact that someone asks the question is a sign that there's nothing to worry about. When they realise they can have self-worth just for the asking, it's eye-opening. That's when they start to think, why the hell have I been doing myself down all this time? I do have the right to approve of myself.

Once you've claimed a high level of self-worth, the next thing is to protect it. Even at times when you don't live up to your personal standards. Even at times when you are being dragged out by the tide. Whatever the merits or otherwise of what you do.

So, how do you protect the self-worth you've claimed, and hold on to the belief that you are already good enough?

Mindful Self-Compassion

When we turn the volume down on CRITICAL FM, it allows us to hear the inner voice of kindness. We all have a natural capacity for this too. We just need to nurture it. That's where 'mindful self-compassion' comes in. I first heard about it twenty years ago, from a clinical psychologist colleague. I have to confess that everything about it put me off. As a hyperactive extrovert, the notion of sitting still and silent, attempting to be present to the moment, seemed like an utter waste of time. Equally, the idea of being kind to myself when others needed my support was almost repulsive. Today, when self-compassion is the height of fashion, I still find it sometimes gets the same reaction. People who experience the Super-Helper Syndrome can view it as self-indulgence. This is a sad reflection of their inattention to their own needs. They spend all their lives in a problem-solving mode. They never get off the hamster wheel of helping. Self-compassion offers them a different mode: it's gentler, more forgiving and allowing. It has three lenses: self-kindness; seeing your own suffering as human; and mindfulness.

Lens 1: Self-Kindness

Imagine your best friend calls. She is distressed and blaming herself. She's embarrassed to be crying down the phone like this. How do you respond? By saying, 'Stop whingeing. No one wants to hear it!' and hanging up? No, of course not. You listen patiently. You feel her pain and want to console her. You offer soothing words. But ... when you are feeling distressed, how do you treat yourself? You desperately attempt to bury the negative emotions. You tell yourself to pull yourself together. You drag yourself through the day behind a smiling facade. These unhealthy defences (avoidance mindset) only serve to mask how we really feel. Beneath them our distress festers. It's as if we've taken the Golden Rule and turned it inside out – we do unto others far better than we do unto ourselves. In fact, if we did treat others the way we treat ourselves, our friends would rightly drop us. We deserve to give ourselves the tender affection we give to others. That's self-kindness.

The following four spotlights are designed to show you how. Activate your approach mindset and come to them with a sense of playful curiosity.

Spotlight 5.2: *Half Hug*

1. Place one hand on your heart and one hand on your belly.
2. As you breathe, feel the belly rise and fall.
3. Feel the gentle pressure of your hands resting here. Notice if there's any warmth.
4. Bring to the Half Hug all the gentle love, care and tenderness that you would if you were hugging one of the people most dear to you in this world.
5. Hold yourself in this safe, secure embrace for about fifteen seconds.

You can use the Half Hug whenever you need to connect with yourself. It can bring calm when you are anxious. It can reassure you in times of self-doubt. It only takes a few moments so can be done anywhere, anytime. If you are struggling in a stressful meeting you can nip out to the loo for a quick Half Hug!

Red flag alert! One thing that can happen when you place your hand on your belly is thoughts like 'My belly is too big' or 'I'm fat'. Isn't that ironic? It's the opposite of self-kindness. The inner critic just won't leave us alone. If that happens to you it's a golden opportunity to practise the decentering exercise: 'I'm having the thought that ...'

Spotlight 5.3: *Breathing in Kindness*

This exercise takes ten minutes. You might want to set a timer so that you can immerse yourself in the experience.

1. Choose one word from the list below that represents the kindness you need right now.
2. Sit in a comfortable position with your feet flat on the floor and your hands resting in your lap.
3. Close your eyes or let your gaze fall unfocused on the floor in front of you.
4. Become conscious of your breathing and then take three deeper breaths.
5. For the following breaths, on each inhalation breathe in the word you've chosen, saying it silently in your head. Connect with the full and deepest meaning of the word and everything it has to bring to you right here and now.
6. Allow it to fill you as the breath fills you.
7. On each exhalation, as you let go of the word, allow yourself to sink into the seat beneath you, feeling supported and safe.
8. On each inhalation draw the word in deeper, filling your whole body.

Energy	Kindness
Confidence	Excitement
Curiosity	Clarity
Encouragement	Wisdom
Compassion	Inspiration
Freedom	Power

You could choose a different word for Breathing in Kindness each day. You can adapt the time to what works for you. If you have identified a particular activating event that triggers your inner critic, you could use Breathing in Kindness to help prepare for it. Choose a word that represents how you want to feel at that time.

Spotlight 5.4: *Self-Kindness Invocation*

When you are feeling low on energy, read this aloud slowly.

In this moment, allowing myself to feel however I feel,
acknowledging the tiredness in my body,
my mixed emotions and my jumble of thoughts,
I offer to myself warmth in the cold, soft light in the darkness,
calm in the chaos, tender strength to lift myself up,
and the courage to carry on.

Lens 2: You're Only Human

It's human to suffer. At a rational level we all know this. But paradoxically, when we are in the grip of our emotions, we forget it. We tell ourselves we shouldn't be suffering. It's ironic that people who are so full of compassion for others are so lacking in compassion for themselves. What is called for here is to look through the second lens of mindful self-compassion: to see the humanity of our own suffering. To build a sense of unconditional self-worth means to be charitable to ourselves. Sometimes you can't bring an end to your own suffering any more than you could for anyone else. But you can offer yourself understanding and love – be your own shoulder to cry on.

Spotlight 5.5: *Self-Approval Affirmation*

This makes use of a phrase adapted from one used in some other therapies. Use it when you start blaming yourself or reverting to negative self-evaluation. Identify the specific thought and insert it into the following phrase:

Even though _____, I deeply and completely love and approve of myself.

Here's an example:

Even though I feel highly anxious today, I deeply and completely love and approve of myself.

It can be cathartic to work through a whole string of these – they don't even have to make sense. It's surprising how they bubble up once you start:

Even though I feel highly anxious today, and I can't believe I snapped at the shop assistant, and feel really bad about that, and I don't think this compassion stuff is working, I deeply and completely love and approve of myself.

If you tried the Self-Approval Affirmation, did you experience any resistance? This might be difficult to do the first few times. It can feel like the clothes don't fit, but keep going with it. When I first tried it I felt awkward at the idea of telling myself that I deeply and completely love and approve of myself. I found it hard to think of any thoughts to include. But now it's one of the exercises I use most frequently. It's a brilliant little de-shamer.

The following exercise can be used anytime you lose the connection to your own humanity. You could memorise some of the phrases (or take a photo of them). Saying them aloud to yourself can reassure and soothe you when you are suffering. You can also recite them silently at challenging times when you are caring for someone else.

Spotlight 5.6: *Forgiveness for Self-Judgement*

Say the phrases below to yourself as you would kind-heartedly talk to a friend who is being tough on themselves:

Sorry you are beating yourself up at the moment ... I know that it's tough for you right now ... I know that you are suffering ... Allow yourself to feel however you feel ... And know that I am here for you ... We all judge ourselves unfairly at times ... I care for you ... you are already good enough.

This can also work well if you record it on your phone. That way you can play the recording back even when you are so caught up in self-judgement that you can't bring yourself to read the words.

Lens 3: Mindfulness

Looking through the third lens of mindful self-compassion allows us to be present on purpose in the moment. To turn towards uncomfortable feelings rather than trying unsuccessfully to back away from them. Instead of the inner critic dragging us on a god-forsaken journey, rehearsing the same old dramatic storyline, mindfulness brings us back to what's happening here and now.

There are two parallel paths to a more mindful life. The first is by learning to pay attention to what's going on moment by moment every day. You deliberately notice your thoughts and feelings. You bring yourself back to awareness whenever you find you have been tangled up in your internal world. You use your breath, your body or the physical environment to ground you. You allow yourself to be with your current state, whatever that may be, rather than trying to change it. Over time you become an astute observer, catching irrational thoughts as they arise. Over time they lose their power. This doesn't just happen; it develops from a conscious choice to commit to a life of mindfulness.

The second path is to adopt a formal practice to support you on your daily path. This involves various types of meditation. There's a growing body of evidence to show that they can bring health benefits. When you meditate regularly you gradually become more calm and more mindful, even at times of the day when you aren't meditating. If you want to make this part of your lifestyle, it's a good idea to take a training course. As well as teaching you to meditate, a course will reinforce your appreciation that thoughts are just mental events; they aren't reality or the truth.

Occasionally people I've worked with have found the idea of meditation difficult because they say they aren't good at emptying their minds. But mindfulness meditations don't ask you to do that. Instead, you train yourself to bring your attention back to a focal point (often the breath) whenever it wanders off. I've provided a meditation for you to try, written out in full below. You can also listen to the recorded version at www.jessbaker.co.uk/shs.

Spotlight 5.7: *Mindful Breathing*

Find a quiet place to do this ten-minute exercise. You might want to set a timer so that you can immerse yourself in the experience.

Sit in a comfortable position with your feet flat on the floor and your hands resting in your lap.

Close your eyes or let your gaze fall unfocused on the floor in front of you.

Become conscious of your breathing and then take three deeper breaths.

Become aware of the sensations as the air passes through your nose.

Notice the sensation of the breath passing down into your belly.

Become aware of your belly rising as you breathe in and falling as you breathe out.

When your mind wanders, which it will, gently bring your attention back to the breath.

This breath ... and this breath.

There's nothing to be or do here. Just breathing.

Allow the body to breathe however it wants to.

However many times your mind wanders, gently bring your attention back to the breath.

This breath ... and this breath.

There's nothing to be or do here. Just breathing.

Repeat this for the full ten minutes.

After completing the mindful breathing meditation, reflect on your experience. Did your mind wander? Were you judging yourself? These are normal experiences. The key to mindfulness is practising it. If you do look at my website you will also find the Compassion Stone meditation and the Bringing Gentle Calming Tenderness meditation, which you can do whenever you feel physical discomfort or pain.

Practising mindful self-compassion and taming the inner critic take time and sustained effort. But they are vital, not least because helpers are unreasonably tough on themselves. The interviewees and questionnaire respondents I approached when researching this book gave their time generously. Their input was invaluable. But they frequently queried the adequacy of their answers. 'Is this any use?' 'I'm probably babbling.' 'I hope I'm not wasting your time.' The extent of self-criticism in helpers is painful to witness. The last of those examples is particularly ironic given how busy they all were. There was more risk of me wasting their time. After listing seven specific helping roles, all but one of which were unpaid, one respondent wrote, 'I don't really consider myself to be a helpful person.' So, before we move on to tackle the second of the irrational beliefs, here's a quick reminder to be kinder to yourself. You can use the exercise below whenever you are being overly self-critical. It's also a fun one to do with children.

Spotlight 5.8: *Self-Compassion Energiser*

1. Stand with your feet hip-width apart and your arms hanging by your sides.
2. Close your eyes if you feel safe to do so.
3. Become aware of the breath.
4. On the next in-breath, take a deep breath and clench the body as much as you can – every muscle in each limb, screw up your face, raise your shoulders to your ears, curl your fingers and toes.
5. At the same time, clench your mind, gripping all the negative thoughts and judgements about yourself, holding them in.
6. Hold this tension for six seconds.
7. As you release the breath, release all the tension that has accumulated in your mind and body. Give yourself a moment to bring kindness and support to yourself. Allow your body to relax into the knowledge that you are already good enough.

Chapter 6

The Help Everyone Belief

Surrounded by mountains, far from nowhere, our friends have a cottage in Wales. There's no internet and no phone signal. That's why we have come here for a few days to work on Chapter 6 of the book. It's late now. The end of a long day writing. The fire is burning down. The clock clicks. Nothing else breathes. If I were to take you out the back door and up the steep grass into the night, I'd show you the sheer quantity of stars. I've always known they were out there but here I can see every one. They are all about, some touching the tops of the hills, others high overhead. And if I were to show you the transcripts of my interviews you might have a similar experience. You would be in awe at the infinite quantity of helping.

Take the photographer I mentioned when I first introduced the idea of a compulsion to help. She was helping in nineteen different ways. That wasn't a record. For the people I spoke to, doing more than was required to care for their customers, clients or patients was just a starting point. They were supporting colleagues both at work and in their personal time. They had a queue of people who were emotionally dependent on them. They were the fixers in their families, the ones that everyone turned to, providing either general support or sharing their expertise. If they had children they were invariably looking after other people's children too, and even their pets. They played a key role in the PTA and organising the activities their children took part in. They were offering advice to all and sundry. They gave away their resources and lent money they couldn't afford. They volunteered time they didn't have for local causes. They were forever fundraising for charities. They looked out for elderly or vulnerable neighbours. They ferried people to hospital and doctors' appointments or picked up their medication. They stopped to assist strangers in the street. It was hard not to conclude that they were trying to help everyone.

Spotlight 6.1: *Who Are You Helping?*

Look back at Spotlight 3.1, listing the types of helping you do. Write down everyone you can think of who you've helped in the past three weeks – include your ongoing helping relationships and any examples of impromptu help you've offered. Keep adding to this list, as we will refer back to it.

It is understandable to want to do what we can to alleviate the suffering of others. Any reasonable person would agree. It's only unhealthy if we start to take personal responsibility to help everyone we meet. Everyone else's problem becomes your problem. The thinking becomes irrational when we believe 'I *should* help everyone'. This is the second tyrannical self-instruction that lights the fire under compulsive helpers. If we slot it into the Activation–Belief–Consequence model, the activating event is seeing someone else with a problem, the belief is I should help everyone, and the consequence is compulsive helping. But it's done before you know it. As with other irrational beliefs, if you hold the Help Everyone Belief, you're unlikely to be aware of it.

It's Like a Little Clue!

One client, who had cancelled several previous appointments, finally showed up late one afternoon. She said she felt drained. While we talked,

I began to suspect she held the Help Everyone Belief. So I asked her to journal her activity. After protesting she didn't have time to do this, she eventually agreed. About a month later, I received an email in which she had painstakingly logged how she spent her time over one week. It was clear she travelled from early morning to late evening to see patients across several locations, spent hours on calls to long-distance relatives, made in-person visits to elderly family members on the other side of the city, chaired a faith-group meeting and dedicated a few hours to her role as an unpaid professional adviser to the government. All of her activities involved helping. The log didn't detail when she ate, but I assumed she did. The Help Everyone Belief had signed its name on every page. When she could see this for herself, she was shocked and saddened, then ashamed. She said, 'I get it now: I'm a helpaholic.'

It can take someone else to point out that you hold this belief. When we talked about resentment, I mentioned that it's often the partner of the helper who feels it first – a sort of vicarious resentment. Helpers sometimes say that their partner who intervenes to stop them from helping is just an annoyance. But if someone is trying to protect you, this can be a little clue that you hold the Help Everyone Belief. Another signifier might be if you read the examples of the photographer or the woman with the journal and thought, 'That's nothing!' Or, if you thought, 'I don't do as much as that', and criticised yourself for not doing more. If you believe you should help everyone, you've probably experienced at least one of the adverse impacts of the Super-Helper Syndrome: exhaustion, resentment, exploitation and self-criticism. In particular, the Help Everyone Belief is a fast track to exhaustion.

Incurable Fanatics

At this point, there's a distinction that's worth drawing between our compulsive helpers and an even more ambitious sort. The people I have encountered quietly go about helping everyone they meet. This starts with those closest to them: their family, neighbours and friends. Often, but not always, they work in jobs that give them the maximum exposure to those who need help. But in a sense, they are ordinary people. There is little to mark them out from the crowd.

> If to be feelingly alive to the sufferings of my fellow-creatures ... is to be a fanatic. I am one of the most incurable fanatics ever permitted to be at large.
>
> William Wilberforce, in *The Life of William Wilberforce*

By contrast, the other sort is anything but ordinary. They devote their lives to strangers in eye-catching ways. Some give nearly all their money to charity and live in poverty in order to affiliate with the poor. Some set off to work in war zones, facing hardship and danger as part of foreign aid efforts. Some leave their families to start charities in the most deprived parts of the world. Some donate an organ to a stranger, risking their own health. Others set out on a mission to adopt as many children as they can. They have been called 'do-gooders' by the journalist Larissa MacFarquhar, and their gripping and often unsettling life stories are chronicled in her book *Strangers Drowning*. The title refers to how they are the sort of people who, following a thought experiment from utilitarian philosophy, would save two strangers rather than one of their own loved ones because two lives are worth more than one life, even if that is the life of your own child. This is one characteristic that differentiates them from the type of compulsive helpers we are talking about. The do-gooders often show less concern for their own families than for strangers. They live the moral principles of utilitarianism. They believe their duty is to provide the maximum amount of relief to the maximum number of people. Some of them are members of the 'Effective Altruism' movement which seeks to quantify how to do the most good. Its devotees take the highest paid jobs they can find in order to be able to give more money to charity. They agonise over decisions like whether it would be selfish to have children because that would be an unnecessary expense and would reduce the amount of money they have available to donate.

Although I find the idea of do-gooders fascinating, and they are undoubtedly examples of people who help to the detriment of their own wellbeing, they are peripheral to the subject of this book. They are driven by principle rather than compassion. Individual lives, including their own, often matter less to them. Also, I haven't met any of them yet: they are rarer than the compulsive helpers we know.

Empathy in Overdrive

The Help Everyone Belief is linked to a heightened awareness of the needs of other people. The philosopher Kristen Renwick Monroe has a similar idea in her book, *The Heart of Altruism*, which I touched on in the prologue. She sees altruism as resulting from a particular perspective that, 'provides a feeling of being strongly linked to others through a shared humanity'. She sees this as core to altruists' identity, leaving them with no choice in their behaviour. This strong link certainly reminds me of many of the people I spoke to. They don't just have a radar to detect the pain around them, that radar is boosted and the signal is unbearably intense. Every conversation is targeted at drawing out the other person's needs. They scan everyone they meet to discern their suffering. They automatically scan their whole environment. They are driving through town looking for a parking space and get distracted by the sight of their recently widowed neighbour. This sets off an internal reverie, worrying that he must be feeling lonely and sad, wondering how he's doing and whether they should pay him a visit. Then their partner says, 'Why the hell did you just drive past two empty spaces?'

One of the possible reasons for helping investigated by Daniel Batson was whether people could be trying to relieve their distress when they experience the suffering of others – the 'avoid-empathy hypothesis'. He found that this wasn't so when they helped for reasons of compassion. However, when empathy goes into overdrive it could be that people are no longer helping out of compassion, but to relieve their own distress. And that's never going to work because there's always more suffering to be found. With the Good Person Belief you only need to help enough to keep your self-judgements at bay, to satisfy yourself, if only briefly, that you are a good person. The Help Everyone Belief is a more demanding taskmaster. There's no let-up: you should help everyone.

The compulsion to jump in – compulsion feels like the opposite of spaciousness – the rope between you and other people – it's my job to jump in – there's no chance to think or say no.

Social Worker, Interviewee

Remember Martha Nussbaum's three cognitive requirements for us to experience compassion? We need to believe the suffering is a serious bad event; we need to believe it's not the person's fault; and we need to bring that person into our circle of concern (eudaimonistic judgement). With the Help Everyone Belief it seems likely that either the first or the third of these cognitions has gone awry.

One of my interviewees happened upon an old lady who was unconscious, having tripped and bashed her head on a wall. She held her and tried to staunch her bleeding until the ambulance came. 'I've got loads of scenarios like this,' she said, 'do you want to hear more?' In this case, the old lady had clearly suffered a serious bad event. But it's not always so clear-cut. If you constantly respond to every instance of suffering as if someone has bashed their head against a wall, then you have lost the ability to evaluate whether there's really been a serious bad event, one that warrants your compassion.

Julia, stopping to guide the man at the station, was an example. What would have happened if she hadn't helped? Maybe someone else would have stopped and offered to, or maybe he would have sorted out his own travel arrangements or attracted the attention of someone in uniform who was actually paid to guide him. Julia told me that while he was a little confused, he wasn't particularly upset. As she walked him to his platform, he cheerfully told her all about the four grandchildren he was on his way to visit. It certainly wasn't a head-bash scenario.

Another of the interviewees said, 'I don't really have a cut-off point. If somebody needs help, then I should help them, and I can sometimes perceive someone as needing help when they don't.' She went on to say how, at networking events, she feels sorry for anyone she spots on the fringes and makes it her duty to go and introduce them to a few people. In the grand scheme of suffering in the world, standing on the periphery of a social gathering doesn't rank that highly. The person might not be suffering at all. Even if they are, it isn't a serious bad event. When someone holds the

Help Everyone Belief, their hypersensitive empathy is incessantly activated. Again, I'm reminded of the eager smoke alarm in our kitchen.

Moving on with the three requirements for compassion, an alternative possibility is that helpers sometimes make skewed eudaimonistic judgements. In other words, they bring into their circle of concern situations that don't belong there. Even when someone is suffering a serious bad event, there are times when your compassion is not warranted. That's because, as we've seen, compassion is a motivator to help, and sometimes it's not your responsibility to do so. If the ambulance had already arrived and the paramedics were lifting the old lady who had bashed her head onto a stretcher, there would have been no need for my interviewee to intervene. That's straightforward to see. But what if another passer-by had already been tending to the old lady? Sometimes the edges of your responsibility are blurred. Someone with the Help Everyone Belief is likely to jump in, wanting to help the old lady, or help the person who was already assisting her. Their natural response is to believe that there is always something they can do to help. Following Martha Nussbaum's theory, unless they believe they can't help, someone experiencing compassion will be motivated to take action. As one of the interviewees put it, 'I can fall into other's experience too easily.' But in some situations a more passive emotion like sympathy is all that's required – just to walk on by and hope the woman being carried into the ambulance will be okay.

Earlier we touched on the ideas of Paul Bloom, who is against empathy. I disagreed with some of what he said – remember the nurse who enabled a terminally ill patient to have a final cigarette? But Bloom does make some compelling points about how emotional empathy alone can be a bad guide for decision making. When empathy goes into overdrive there's an increased risk of making poor judgements.

When people try to help everyone there's no discrimination. They are busy hearts. In a sense they are at the opposite pole to the Effective Altruists (not that I'm advocating that extreme either). They are ineffective altruists. Instead, they could target their efforts where the need is most acute.

Spotlight 6.2: *Are You Spreading Yourself Too Thin?*

Review your answers to the Compassion Test in Spotlight 2.2 and your lists of helping in Spotlights 3.1 and 6.1, or think about all the examples of helping you've done recently.

Do you ever overreact to suffering when it's really not that bad?

Do you ever jump in to help when it's not your responsibility?

Do you ever jump in to help when it's not appropriate?

Could some of the people you are helping find help elsewhere?

If you answer yes to these questions and have ready examples, it's a strong indication that you hold the Help Everyone Belief. You can use your own examples as a way to analyse the type of judgements that trigger your empathy in overdrive. You can also refer to them when you come to deconstruct the belief.

What Causes the Help Everyone Belief?

One piece of the puzzle appears to be empathy in overdrive. It seems to be a risk factor for the Help Everyone Belief, like high blood pressure being a risk factor for cardiovascular diseases. And the belief, in its turn, is a risk factor for the Super-Helper Syndrome. But that's not enough of an answer. Where does empathy come from in the first place? Why do some people have more than others? And what other factors might drag someone under the sway of this belief?

Cambridge Professor Simon Baron-Cohen has developed a theory of what he (controversially, and to my mind unnecessarily) calls the 'male' and the 'female' brains. According to him, the former is better at 'systemising' and the latter is better at 'empathising'. He refers to evidence from an evolutionary perspective and from neuroscientific studies. While his theory is by no means universally accepted, the idea that some brains are wired for empathising does sound like what we are interested in here. When discussing the 'extreme female brain' he speculates that, 'It is as if their empathy circuit is in a constant state of hyper-arousal, such that other people are never off their radar' – what I'm referring to as empathy in overdrive. He paints a picture of an extremely empathic psychotherapist, who sounds utterly lovely, but is also described as 'virtually technically disabled'. Since Baron-Cohen believes the extreme has to be pathological, he goes on to speculate that, 'Presumably, when someone is so other-focused that they neglect their own basic needs for food, money, and other resources linked to survival, one can talk of pathology'. That does sound like an ultra-virulent strain of the Super-Helper Syndrome. But, while helpers do frequently neglect their own needs, this is rarely to the extent that we would call pathological.

The idea of the 'extreme female brain' also sounds somewhat like Vicki Helgeson's notion of unmitigated communion. I mentioned her theory when we looked at how ignoring your own needs is one of the components of the Super-Helper Syndrome. Those with unmitigated communion 'seem to carry helping behavior to an extreme'. Although Helgeson sees it as a personality trait that is stable over time, she also suggests that it is rooted in environmental events, and therefore can be moderated to some degree. That's good news for anyone wanting to temper their compulsive helping.

It seems that the empathy in overdrive that underlies the Help Everyone Belief does relate to a specific psychological profile. That partly answers the question of why some people have more empathy than others. It also begs the further question: Where does that profile come from?

Is Helping Hereditary?

The first place to look if you want to work out if something is genetically determined is to compare twins. Monozygotic (identical) twins have exactly the same set of genes. Dizygotic (non-identical) twins share only 50 per cent of their genes. But both types typically grow up in similar circumstances to each other with the same socio-economic opportunities. That means that any commonalities found in identical twins that aren't found in non-identical twins can probably be put down to their genes. Scientists have measured empathy in twins using self-report questionnaires. They have also used behavioural measures such as observing children's responses when they watch their mother catching her finger in a suitcase. Ouch. They have found a sizeable genetic component, especially for emotional empathy, estimated at 68 per cent in one study.

Scientists in Baron-Cohen's laboratory have searched for the specific genes involved in the personality trait of empathy. To test all of the 30,000 genes that make a human being would have been like looking for a needle in a very expensive needlestack. Instead, they targeted sixty-eight candidate genes. They measured the personality trait using their Empathy Quotient (EQ) questionnaire. When the genetic material taken from participants was compared with their empathy questionnaire scores, the scientists found, to their delight, that four of the genes they had selected were strongly associated with levels of empathy. Their experiments showed that empathy is determined, to some extent, by our genes.

A heap of evidence that helping has a hereditary component has also been reviewed by Dacher Keltner, of the University of California at Berkeley, and his colleagues. He looked at three circuits in the brain: the attunement system, the caregiving system and the reward system. Genetic variations have been found that affect the neurotransmitters associated with each of these systems: serotonin, oxytocin and dopamine. I'll take a closer peek at that review when we come to look at the healthy helper because those transmitters are also responsible for some of the rewards we get from helping.

If helping systems are hereditary it makes me wonder if the empathy in overdrive that I see in the Super-Helper Syndrome also has a genetic component. Are some people born with hyperactive empathy circuitry that predisposes them to the Help Everyone Belief? And, if so, does that mean they have no choice, that they are pre-programmed that way? That there's no point in fighting it?

Baron-Cohen does acknowledge that empathy is not wholly genetic. He stresses the interaction of genes and the environment in determining our behaviour. And he recognises that a 'high-level construct like empathy' cannot be directly caused by our genes. In a similar way, the sociobiologist Richard Dawkins acknowledges that we don't have to be selfish just because genes are essentially selfish. Equally, we don't have to be at the mercy of our overactive genes for empathy. As rational beings we have the possibility to make choices about how much we help others, when and who we help, and when to ignore the insistent ringtone of our empathy circuitry. Before we look at how to do that, let's consider what those environmental determinants might be.

Turning Trauma Around

My father had done a classic evening of destruction. I could hear it from my bedroom, where I was hiding. I was about 6. When I heard him leave I got out of bed and went to her. She was sitting in the kitchen. It was destroyed and she was crying. I had my book under one arm and my favourite teddy under the other and I said, 'Lets go!' And I remember being just ready, you know. And she looked at me with defeat in her eyes, so of course we didn't go anywhere. And that was the moment where I gave up on her. She wasn't going to help me get out of there. I had to find another way.

Psychologist, Interviewee

The data I've collected point to two ways in which early experience can prime the Help Everyone Belief. The first is that some people metamorphose into helpers as a result of childhood pain. When I asked people why they became a helper, they often referenced their childhood. Many had experienced early deprivation or hardship. Some grew up with volatile or abusive parents. Childhood trauma doesn't necessarily make people into helpers. It sculpts them in many forms. But it does shape compulsive helpers out of some of them. They move on from their trauma to become the problem-solver, the fixer, the go-to rescuer in the family. They move on from trauma to a career as an expert helper.

I idealised my parents, but looking back my mum was hot and cold and it's the cold bits that stick out for me. I was very in-your-face love me love me love me! And I'd get nothing. That rejection stands out for me. It's naturally heightened my awareness of my impact on others. I don't want to upset anyone; I want to do right by them and help people. I think in a way that may have impacted me a little bit.

Dentist, Interviewee

Childhood Messages – Seeing the Suffering

The second possible precursor to the Help Everyone Belief is childhood messages. These play a part in much the same way as they did in the formation of the Good Person Belief. With that irrational belief, the messages trained a child to make judgements about whether they were good or not. With the Help Everyone Belief, the messages relate more to drawing the child's attention to other people's suffering. One woman had an alcoholic father. He had stopped drinking as soon as she was born. He became heavily involved in setting up an alcoholics' support group. He would disappear on errands of mercy in the middle of the night. When she was old enough he would take her on missions to 'go and see the poorly man'. Her deep connection with her father and these formative memories were still with her more than forty years later.

I've just gone back to my data and dug out one of the questionnaires. Here's the answer to the question: How did you become a helper? Uncannily, she starts, 'It's in my DNA.' But then she goes on to write about her childhood:

I grew up in a small rural community and mum, despite being a single parent, was at the heart of it: always helping others – she was a Girl Guide leader, set up a local toddler playgroup, and was at the heart of all activities in the village. She's my role model and inspiration and instilled in me, my brother, and sister, just how important it is to do our duty to help other people (as summed up by the Guide promise!). During winter our village would often get snowed in and lots of lorries and cars would be stuck. We would be out there with flasks of hot tea and soup and sandwiches and making sure people were warm enough, dishing out blankets and sleeping bags. We didn't have much but what we did have we were happy to share.

Healthcare Strategy Consultant, Questionnaire Respondent

A final example comes from one of my colleagues. When he was little it was agonising watching the news with his mother. She'd huff at every report of famine and disaster around the world, scolding the politicians on the television. She was active in many causes. She traipsed door to door for Christian Aid, distributing and collecting donation envelopes. Every Sunday she stood at the back of the cold church in her Clothkits coat, behind a trestle table heaped with bags of Traidcraft coffee. The message he most vividly recalled was whenever her children were impatient for mealtimes. If he, or any of his brothers said, 'I'm starving,' she reproached them. 'Don't say that. There are children starving in Africa.' Her four sons went on to be a nurse, a teacher, a social worker and a psychologist.

In each of these examples the childhood messages are a combination of repeated reminders of suffering, and of being exposed to role models who attempt to alleviate that suffering.

Reasons You Can't Help Everyone

Whether it is in your genetic programming, shaped by early trauma or the product of childhood messages, the belief becomes so deeply ingrained it can be difficult to see why you can't help everyone.

Reason 1: *You Don't Have the Capacity to Help Everyone*
It should be obvious that you don't have the capacity to help everyone. It's so obvious I shouldn't have to write that you don't have the capacity to help everyone. But try telling compulsive helpers they don't have the capacity to help everyone. They run out of time. They run out of energy. Most people

would see these as warnings to slow down, but the compulsive helper sees them as a test. Exhaustion is their normal state. They get frustrated when their overcrowded diary shouts, 'You don't have the capacity to help everyone.' They squeeze in one more request for help when their life is already loaded up like a car on a camping trip. We've seen it in examples like the photographer and the woman who kept a journal. I have folders of interview transcripts like that. Every page of those transcripts says you don't have the capacity to help everyone.

Reason 2: *Caution! You Don't Have the Capability*

The risk of trying to help beyond your capability should be included in the safety precautions that come with information help. We've already discussed the propensity to give ready advice. None of us has the information, qualifications or specialist knowledge to resolve every situation. For instance, if your friend is in dispute with a builder over a substandard extension to their kitchen what they might need is a lawyer. When you refer them on to a specialist, that in itself is helping. If you hold the Help Everyone Belief, it can be tough when you realise you don't have the skills to help.

This reminds me of a woman I met who was always dishing out titbits of nutritional advice. Everyone at the table would be told which combinations of food they should or shouldn't eat. She was trying to be helpful, but much of what she said sounded anecdotal. It felt awkward when, at one networking lunch, she was placed next to the head of nutrition and dietetics from the local NHS trust.

Insecurities about their capability can lead compulsive helpers to exaggerated behaviour. They amass a collection of helper skills. They could cover their walls with a gallery of framed certificates: another telltale sign of the Help Everyone Belief. When one woman came to me, she was already a family solicitor, a qualified yoga teacher and was studying an online aromatherapy course. Although she felt stretched, she was also about to embark on training to be a counsellor. She showed me some of her client feedback. The positive reviews she received didn't satiate her thirst to help more people, more of the time, in more ways.

Reason 3: *Your Help Isn't Needed – It's Not Your Task*

When you are a psychologist interviewing people, for the many reasons we do, there's something that sometimes happens at the end, after you have finished your questions. People relax out of their I-am-being-interviewed mode into a more informal conversational mode. This can be the moment when they open up or their most colourful examples come to mind. It was as one of those afterthoughts that a nurse told me this story. She was outside the leisure centre chatting to her gym-buddy before getting into her car. Across the car park she caught sight of a lady halfway out of her car seat, struggling with the open door. She was parked in a disabled bay. The nurse raced over and said, 'Let me help you.' She hooked her arm under the lady's and used her body to gently lift her from the car. The lady didn't say anything until she was almost hauled out. Then she told the nurse she had actually been trying to get in. The nurse said how sorry she was, but the lady didn't seem to mind. Although this was recounted to me as a funny afterthought, it nicely illustrates how your help sometimes isn't needed. It also shows how empathy in overdrive can lead to poor judgements.

In the same way that it was obvious that you don't have the capacity to help everyone, for a variety of reasons, it should also be obvious that sometimes your help is not required. Remember the definition in Chapter 1 – for it to be help, it has to be needed. But again, the instinct to help can kick in before a compulsive helper has even questioned it. Might the person already know where they can find a solution? Might they already be getting help from elsewhere?

A useful concept here is the 'separation of life tasks' as identified by Alfred Adler in his theory of Individual Psychology. Adler stressed the importance of identifying what is, and what is not, your responsibility. A classic example is when 'helping' a child to do their homework. According to Adler's idea, it's the child's task not the parent's. Forcing them to study can just lead to frustration and resentment in both the parent and the child. Establishing the separation of tasks would be to make it clear that it's the child's responsibility, and why. Then, not to offer more help than the child wants. Adler pointed out that we are constantly trying to take responsibility for how other people behave. When you start to notice this, you are likely to find yourself doing it all the time. When I first moved in with Rod and his son, I found myself picking up wet towels from the bathroom floor. After a while I felt resentful that I was doing this. Then I thought, they must have eventually picked up the towels before I moved in, and nobody had asked me to pick them up. It wasn't my task, so I stopped. When your help is not required it can be liberating to pause and remind yourself, 'It's not my task.'

Even if you are highly empathic, you can't always know exactly what other people need. Sometimes there isn't even a problem to be solved. That's when the compulsive helper can be tempted to go digging around, trying to unearth one. The risk is that others perceive this as meddling. It's one possible side effect of the Help Everyone Belief.

Reason 4: *Your Help Isn't Wanted*

If you believe you should help everyone, it can be disheartening to acknowledge that some people just don't want your help. This can be for myriad reasons to do with the psychological state of the person, or the relationship you have with them. Writing this section reminds me of a little incident when I went to dinner at my friend's flat to meet his girlfriend. After I helped her clear the plates, I started doing the washing up. It was my way of making a contribution and to say thank you for the delicious lasagne. When I got to scrubbing the pans she turned to me, 'Can you stop! You're making me feel like I have a dirty home.' I've just noticed that this and all of the other examples in this section on Reasons You Can't Help Everyone, from giving nutritional advice to hauling women out of cars to picking up wet towels, are assumptive rather than responsive help. A tendency to give assumptive help when it's not wanted is one of the perils of trying to help everyone.

Some people do need help but aren't ready to be helped yet, for psychological reasons. They might say, 'I just can't face this at the moment.' Dealing with the issue right now can feel like breaking open Pandora's Jar. In more extreme cases, there are people who will never be ready. They are not just beyond your help, but beyond help full stop. They can be a magnet for the compulsive helper. One of my psychologist friends spent months on the phone to one of his own friends, a guy who kept splitting up and getting back together with his girlfriend. The guy repeatedly acknowledged he was being given good advice. 'Yeah, yeah, you're right. That's what I should do.'

But he seldom did anything about it, and when he did, he quickly relapsed, putting everything back at square one. Of course, sometimes it's enough to be a pillow to cry on. On other occasions, like with the guy above, you might initially feel you're helping but in the long run nothing changes. Meanwhile, these missions divert your energy from those who do actually want your help.

The quality of the relationship also dictates who you can or cannot help. People more readily accept help from those they like, are familiar with and, especially, trust. Despite all that, it may simply be that, lovely as you are, some of those you want to help don't feel you are the right person. It can hurt when you find out you are not the chosen helper.

Another reason your help may not be wanted is because accepting help often requires the disclosure of personal information. This is a subtle area with many pitfalls. Helpers, especially those who subscribe to the Help Everyone Belief, naturally ask a swarm of questions. But in order to be certain that their help is wanted, they need to tune in to how guarded each potential helpee is, and their threshold for privacy. It makes me think of the radio psychiatrist in Nora Ephron's movie, *Sleepless in Seattle*. Jonah, Tom Hanks's son, phones in to her show without his knowledge. Dr Marcia eventually speaks to the reticent father, and after claiming that she doesn't want to invade his privacy asks, live on air, 'How long ago did your wife die?'

The very fact that you are giving expert help in a professional setting can also determine how much people are prepared to disclose. Patients, clients or service users are more likely to confide in you about other aspects of their lives. This crops up too for organisational psychologists brought in to improve business performance. Employees in the client organisation can start to open up about details of their personal lives because they know they are speaking to a psychologist. Depending on the exact situation – the type of help you are being employed to provide, how much time you have available and your remit – this can be a challenge for the compulsive helper.

In the first chapter I explored the role of status as part of the dynamics of helping relationships. Some people don't want to ask for your help because, for them, it would create a status imbalance. Even if the offer of help is from the heart, out of compassion, with no expectation of reciprocity, it can be turned down because the other person doesn't want to feel a sense of indebtedness. This intrinsically unbalanced nature of the helping relationship can go deeper. For some, there's an element of shame attached to asking for help. Brené Brown, who writes about courage and vulnerability, defines shame as 'the intensely painful feeling or experience of believing that we are flawed and therefore unworthy of love, belonging, and connection'. Unfortunately, acknowledging the need for help can trigger this cruel and self-defeating emotion. That's another reason people don't ask for help, even when they really need it, and it's another reason why, sadly ... you can't help everyone.

Help isn't possible in any of the situations we've just looked at: you don't have the capacity, you don't have the capability, your help isn't needed, your help isn't wanted. None of them meet the definition I started from: make something easier or possible for someone by offering them resources, information, expertise and, or, support, when they both want and need this. You might remember Professor Barbara Oakley, who I mentioned when we first looked at the idea of helpers not meeting their own needs. Whenever a person attempts to help everyone, they run the risk of becoming what she defines as a 'pathological altruist':

> A person who sincerely engages in what he or she intends to be altruistic acts, but who harms the very person or group he or she is trying to help, often in unanticipated fashion; or harms others; or irrationally becomes a victim of his or her own altruistic actions.

And who wants that? Let's deconstruct the belief.

Deconstructing the Help Everyone Belief

Acknowledge You HOLD the Belief

When faced with the idea of this belief, people start by saying it sounds a bit extreme, I don't try to help everyone! But when they review their compulsive helping behaviour they come to the realisation that they're living by the rule 'I should help everyone'.

You may have already come to a conclusion about whether you hold this belief. Maybe a friend or partner who loves you has been trying to point it out for ages. If you haven't decided, I suggest you go back and review Spotlights 3.1, 6.1 and 6.2. What does the evidence tell you?

If you are still unsure whether you hold the belief, you could try asking yourself the following questions. When was the last time you said no to a request for help? When did you last see the need for help and didn't respond?

There's an alternative reaction some people have. They wear the belief like a badge. They see themselves as a super-hero, rescuing the world. I'll come back to the idea of helper's pride. In the meantime, if this is you, what's going to be important is to concede that the belief is both irrational and harmful.

EXPOSE the Belief as Irrational

You can't help everyone – trust me, I've tried! But I hope the previous sections provide enough arguments to convince you that the belief is irrational. If you are still clinging on to it, take a look at the harmful effects.

EXPOSE the Belief as Harmful

If you're a worn-out helper, it could be because you hold the Help Everyone Belief. Trying to help everyone inevitably ends up in physical or mental exhaustion. As we saw earlier, this belief is a demanding taskmaster. You can never relax.

Because it often leads to assumptive helping, others might perceive you as interfering. One unpleasant knock-on effect is that people can start to avoid you. This can also happen when people experience an imbalance in the principle of reciprocity. If you spend all your time helping others but will never accept help in return, it can leave them feeling uncomfortable around you. Or it can go the other way. If you are indiscriminate in who you try to help, you can end up with an entourage of exploiters.

Yet another harmful effect of trying to help everyone is that it can distract you from your own needs, and even from acknowledging your own pain. All your attention is directed at others. This theme is central to the Super-Helper Syndrome. I will come back to it when we look at meeting your own needs.

LET GO of the Belief

When the woman who kept the journal realised that she held the Help Everyone Belief she was shocked and saddened, then ashamed. It's not uncommon to have a range of different emotions. The inner critic can also get in on the story when you resolve to let go of the belief. Typically, it might start broadcasting thoughts like: 'don't be so selfish'; 'people out there need you'; 'you should do something about the suffering in the world'; 'you don't want to become lazy and self-centred'.

But, and you might have heard me say this before, I am not trying to stop you from helping anyone. I'm just trying to stop you from helping everyone! I want your helping to be more sustainable. And, in the case of the Help Everyone Belief, to make your contribution more effective by concentrating your efforts where the need is greatest. If you do experience any backchat from the inner critic, you could revisit the sections on that and self-compassion in Chapters 4 and 5.

If you have decided to let go of the belief, you might be wondering what you are going to do when you're not compulsively helping ...

PUT Something in its Place

An alternative and more rational belief to adopt is 'I know and respect the limits of my capacity to help'. That can be a powerful and liberating perspective. The next challenge is to change your behaviour; that takes practice and dedication. Trying to help everyone is a hard habit to break. Here are a few spotlights to support you.

Spotlight 6.3: *Life Beyond the Help Everyone Belief*

When you're caught in the whirlwind of busyness it's hard to imagine how life could be different. Take a quiet moment to follow this short visioning exercise.

Imagine it's one year from now. You've let go of the belief. You have your compulsive helping well under control.

Where are you? How do you feel?

How are you spending your days?

How are you spending your evenings and weekends?

Who are you enjoying more time with?

Spotlight 6.4: *Pause And Think (PAT)*

This exercise helps you to identify the gap between spotting someone in need of help (the activating event) and helping them (the consequence). It's in this gap that your belief kicks in, I *should* help.

Next time you feel the urge to jump in and help, follow these three steps:

1. Press your own pause button for four seconds, counting in your head: 'Pause, two, three, four.'
2. Remind yourself, for four seconds, you have options: 'And, two, three, four.'
3. Consider your options and choose your behaviour: 'Think, two, three, four.'

In the Pause And Think gap, rather than following the automatic thoughts, you give your rational mind a chance to intervene. With practice you can train yourself to be more deliberate in your actions. You might still choose to help, but at least now you are doing so consciously.

Spotlight 6.5: *Strong Statements*

This exercise is adapted from one used in Rational Emotive Behaviour Therapy (REBT). The aim is to use statements that grip you powerfully at an intellectual and emotional level. You simply read them to yourself as if you believe them. If you are letting go of the Help Everyone Belief this can be a challenge and you may need to come back and spend time with the statements:

'I don't have to help anyone ever.'
'My emotional reaction to others' needs does not govern my behaviour.'
'Even when I have a strong empathic reaction, I know I don't have to act upon it.'
'I have the strength to stay within the limits of my capacity to help.'
'I know when it's not my responsibility to help.'
'I have the absolute right to choose when to help and when not to.'

Alternative Routes to Becoming a Compulsive Helper

The two beliefs we have covered so far are alternative routes to a similar destination. Some compulsive helpers hold one, and some hold both. One way to differentiate them is to consider that the Good Person Belief is internally focused: it's a judgement about your own self-worth. In contrast, the Help Everyone Belief is externally focused: it's a judgement about what's going on around you and what you *should* do about that.

Another way to differentiate them is to view the Good Person Belief as being about why you help (to see yourself as good), and the Help Everyone Belief as being about who you help (everyone). If you hold either of them, you end up on the road to compulsive helping. But there's one more way to get there ...

Chapter 7

They Couldn't Survive
Without Me

I watched *Poltergeist* when it first came out on television, when I was 7. It's a paranormal story about a little girl who disappears from her family. The Chicago Film Critics Association lists it as the twentieth scariest movie of all time. I don't recommend it. I stay away from horror movies these days. But when I was young, I was allowed to stay up late to watch them with my mother. She liked to have me sleep in her bed afterwards. There was a tiny doll hung from my bedroom ceiling. It was a witch on a broomstick, dressed in black. Whenever I asked my mother to take it down, she refused. I would wake in the night and see it and come into her room. She liked it when I was ill and stayed home from school, when I had the headaches. She used to say, 'We're a team.' For as long as I can remember, she said that. 'There are givers and takers in this world, Jessie. Don't be a taker!' The last four words were louder: a threat. She spat out her demands for service. Go upstairs for a pack of cigarettes from the big duty-free box in the wardrobe. Fetch her slippers. Empty the ashtray. If I ever said no to any of her requests she would blow up. If you don't do it, next time you ask me to do something I'm going to say no. She reminded me, 'Make sure you buy me flowers for Mothering Sunday.' Her birthdays were important events. I would bake a cake and make a card and make a fuss. If I didn't, she would be furious. She worked in the accounts department as an administrator with British Gas, but she had periods off work when she would lie in bed. They were her nervous breakdowns. She had palpitations and sciatica. I fetched and carried for her. When I was 10, she took her boss to an employment tribunal. She told me she was being sexually harassed. She asked me what she should say at the tribunal. I said she should tell the truth. When she had a doctor's appointment, she would take me along to the surgery and I would ask the questions. I'd ask about her antidepressant medication, what the side effects were. At the age of 12 I got a babysitting job and she would charge me the price of a taxi to come and collect me. I walked home in the dark instead. Sometimes I would run out of the house crying. I'd run to my childminder, Auntie Jean. My mother would drive along kerb-crawling me, screaming out of the window, 'Get back to the house now!' When I told her I was going to Auntie Jean's she would give up and drive home.

Poltergeist was a film that stuck with me, not just because it's terrifying, but because it was about a little blonde girl. I was a little blonde girl. The actress who played the main character was born one month after me. She died six years later.

There's a third variant of compulsive helping that comes with its own irrational belief. To be honest, I only included it well into my research, after I had formulated the other aspects of the Super-Helper Syndrome. My initial interest was in the type of person I'd seen trying to help everyone. But this other type of helping kept cropping up even though people were uncomfortable talking about it. Perhaps I was reluctant too.

Instead of helping everyone, this variant is limited to helping one person or one small group. It plays out in the context of a particular sort of relationship – caring for those who are dependent. For that reason, it's important to point out what I'm not saying. Of course, it's vital to care for dependent relatives or loved ones. And, of course, helping is fine when it's not detrimental to the wellbeing of the helper: where they look after their own needs too. As you've definitely heard me say before, I'm not trying to stop people giving valuable help. And, in this chapter, I'm not trying to stop you from caring for those you love.

> At the time we began dating he was awaiting renal transplant. I knew he was my soulmate and that I would be there for his surgery and recovery. I was determined to be by his side from start to finish. We lived with his father, his kidney donor, and I would look after them both after the fact. I had absolutely no idea what it entailed. I felt myself distancing from my work, personal goals, and depriving myself of any kind of happiness. I stopped any physical activity because I was exhausted, and subsequently gained weight. I cared for him as best I could. Whatever had to be done, I would do. But I would cry in the bathroom most nights when he was asleep. I was feeling emotionally used and empty.
>
> Freelance Illustrator, Questionnaire Respondent

Only you can decide who you want to help and how much you want to help. If you are caring for someone who is dependent on you then only you can know how much they need your help. If you are in such a relationship with someone you love, then this chapter might be challenging to read. It might trigger some strong reactions. For that reason, the whole chapter comes with an avoidance mindset red flag warning. I'm not judging your relationships, but I do want to provide the framework for you to think about them objectively. And please don't blame yourself if you recognise some of the patterns of behaviour here. If you are caring for a dependant out of love, you might need to remind yourself of that. You might need to go back and look at the spotlights on self-compassion to direct some of that love at yourself. But what comes next is what nobody tells you. If you are in an unhealthy helping relationship with a dependant then it's unlikely that anyone points this out. Other people are more likely to just say how wonderful you are and that your dependant is lucky to have you. As a coach, I want to call out the fact that while this may be true, there may be more to be said.

There are helpers who are trapped in helping relationships which are not healthy. For them, there is a belief that sucks them into compulsive helping: the They-Couldn't-Survive-Without-Me Belief. This is different from the other two beliefs that lead to compulsive helping. The Good Person Belief and the Help Everyone Belief attach themselves to helpers for their whole lives, until they attempt to deconstruct them in the ways we've discussed. Those beliefs are always present in the background, influencing people's behaviour whenever opportunities to help arise. This third belief is different. It's a role that people find themselves playing. It's a belief about someone else: the dependant. As a note on terminology, in this chapter I've used the word 'dependant' to indicate the one or more people being helped. I've referred to CS relationship (i.e., Couldn't Survive relationship) to indicate helping relationships where one party is dependent. I chose CS relationship intending it to be a neutral term. It's not for me to prejudge or generalise about whether these relationships are healthy or not.

When someone is in an unhealthy CS relationship, it's hard for them to accept that the underlying belief is irrational. People start objecting, 'But they couldn't survive without me!' Hence the red flag warning. This chapter carries us into the darker parts of the Super-Helper Syndrome. To expose the belief as irrational we have to explore the shadow-sides of the psyche of the helper and of the dependant. If you already feel unsettled, it might be because you are one of the people this chapter was written for. A strong emotional reaction can make it difficult to examine your motivation for helping and the health of your relationships. You're going to need to switch on your approach mindset. And there is warm light on the other side. We'll soon be talking about how to look after yourself, set effective boundaries and live the compassionate life.

There are three defining criteria that make up the They-Couldn't-Survive-Without-Me Belief:

1. The helper is indispensable. The helper must believe there's nobody else with the capability and the availability to provide the care their

dependant needs. Or they must feel indispensable because the dependant won't accept help from anyone else.

2. Total dependency. The helper must believe that the dependant is unable to care for themselves. They must believe that if the dependant didn't receive their help, there would be extreme consequences: the dependant would collapse or die.

3. The helper has no choice. Whether they are willing or unwilling to be in the relationship, the helper has to believe they can't leave it.

Since each of these is part of the definition, deconstructing this belief as irrational is only possible if you can prove that at least one of these criteria is untrue.

Any CS relationship is an example of extreme dependency-oriented help, pretty much by definition. The belief shuts out the possibility of autonomy-oriented help. CS relationships are also characterised by the helper subjugating their own needs. It feels like part of the duty of care is to put the dependent person first. It would be a dereliction of that duty if the helper were to attend to their own needs.

> Whenever we've booked a holiday I've never looked forward to it because I'm worried about her; what if x or y happens while I'm away. I'm not going to be able to come back at a moment's notice and I know that causes her anxiety. So I never feel that enthusiastic about holidays.
>
> Interviewee

CS relationships occur where the helper is relied upon for either physical or psychological reasons. Examples that readily come to mind are looking after a child with Down's syndrome, a grandfather who has had a stroke, a partner injured in a car accident. As I mentioned earlier, there are an estimated 6.5 million unpaid carers in the UK alone. Dependent relationships can also occur in the workplace. They are found across all occupations, where someone believes their patients, customers or the rest of the team couldn't survive without them. One example would be the story of the boy and the cobbler.

The Boy and the Cobbler

Once there was a boy who came from a poor family. His father died and his mother sent him out to work for the cobbler who made all the shoes for the town. The old man told him to stay in the shop and serve the people when they came in to buy shoes. The old man spent his days in the workshop at the back making new shoes. He told the boy, 'Don't you steal my money, boy! I know how many shoes I make. Don't you steal my money, boy!' The boy sold the shoes and at the end of the week the old man gave him his ha'penny. He took it home to his mother. But there were only a few shoes to sell and soon the shop was bare. He begged the old man to teach him to make shoes and eventually the old man agreed. The boy spent his days with the old man in the workshop making shoes. Whenever the little bell over the shop door tinkled, he ran into the shop to serve the people. But sometimes he worked so hard, he didn't hear the bell. Then the people would steal the shoes. The old man boxed his ears. Some weeks he didn't get his ha'penny. The old man said, 'Don't you steal my money, boy! I know how many shoes I make. Don't you steal my money, boy!' The people in the town complained all day that there weren't enough shoes. They complained all day that their shoes were worn out. The boy couldn't make enough. The old man hardly made any at all. He spent his days fussing over the ledger. He told the boy business was hard. He might lose the shop. The boy begged the old man to let him make shoe repairs as well and eventually the old man agreed. The boy spent his days with the old man in the workshop making and repairing shoes. Whenever the little bell over the shop door tinkled, he ran into the shop to serve the people. But now he spent long hours in the workshop, now he had to repair shoes as well as make new ones. He missed the bell and the people would steal more shoes. The old man boxed his ears and said, 'Don't you steal my money, boy! I know how many shoes I make. Don't you steal my money, boy!' On Saturday afternoons, the old man took the pennies to the money keeper. He came back to the shop with a ticket from the money keeper and wrote the number in the ledger. The boy looked at the tickets and the number didn't match the number of pennies he'd handed over to the old man. He begged the old man to let him take the pennies to the money keeper and eventually the old man agreed.

The old man said, 'Don't you steal my money, boy! I know how many shoes we make.' On Saturday afternoons the boy took the pennies to the money keeper. By now he was bigger than the money keeper. He counted the pennies out on the bench. He checked the tickets. But while he was away the people stole more shoes. The old man boxed his ears. The boy made shoes. He repaired shoes. He took the pennies to the money keeper. He wrote the numbers in the ledger with the old man standing close at his shoulder. He took his ha'penny back to his mother. One day, as he was walking home through the town, he met a man with a long coat and a tall hat. The man said, 'I've been watching you. You make fine shoes. You make fine repairs.' The man looked down at his own pair. They were so shiny the boy could see his own reflection. The man said, 'You're a man now. I have a shop. You can rent it. You'll do well. Think about it. Here's my calling card.' The boy went home and told his mother. His mother said, 'What will you do?' The boy said, 'What would the cobbler do?'

How Dependent Relationships Come About

Dependencies can arise suddenly and unexpectedly. During a time when I was working in a community hospital, a friend and colleague was an occupational therapy assistant. Carol and her husband were six months away from retirement overseas. He was a builder and planned to build them a house on a plot of land they had bought. Then he had a stroke. When he got out of hospital he was practically immobile. He gave up hope of walking again. He had been a powerfully built man and wouldn't let anyone else see him in that weakened state. Carol had to delay her retirement and extend her contract at work. Every night she made him do the rehabilitation exercises he hated. Through her efforts and determination, over a couple of years, eventually he was able to walk with the use of a frame.

In situations where people fall into a CS relationship through no fault of their own, it's plain that the helper is required to disrupt their own life too. But even though we all recognised that Carol was devoted to and had a responsibility towards her husband, I remember the discussions in the staffroom. She would openly talk about the exhaustion that we could all see. I secretly questioned whether she really needed to do everything herself.

CS relationships don't always come about abruptly. People can also slide into one over time. This can happen inexorably as a result of old age or chronic illness. Dementia is probably the most frequent example. In the UK there are around 280,000 people who care for someone with dementia twenty-four hours a day. A coaching client of mine had a mother with Alzheimer's who refused to go into a nursing home. Even when my client was putting her own life on hold and going in before and after work and at weekends to cook, clean and care for her. Even when the doctor said her mother needed professional carers throughout the day and night. Even when her mother would sit alone all day doing nothing, having lost interest in the puzzles that used to fill her hours. The last thing my client wanted was to put her mother into a home, but one of the reasons she came to see me was because of the impact this was having on her own life. She was struggling with the workload in her finance job. In situations like this it's natural for the helper to overlook their own needs.

Sliding into a CS relationship can also come about when there is a gradual change in the dynamics. This happens imperceptibly as both people grow accustomed to the imbalance. It's like how the light can slowly dim when you are reading in the evening. In the story of the boy and the cobbler, neither of them set out to have a dependent relationship. We are told that eventually the old man agreed to each of the boy's suggestions to take on more responsibility. Earlier I mentioned how reciprocity is important in all relationships; over time reciprocity can be eroded. This can be the fate of marital relationships where one person ends up habitually doing everything for the other. When people fall or slide into a CS relationship, the third of the criteria listed above feels true – the helper has no choice.

I was in an abusive relationship and when I sought to end it, both my mother and his said I should help him and stick by him ... I had to argue quite fiercely, what about MY health, and that of my daughter. It showed me that I was surrounded by women who, as wives, believed I should help my husband at all costs.

Questionnaire Respondent

You Let Go of My Hand

Some people are prone to believing that others couldn't survive without them. The most obvious candidates are those who already hold the Good Person Belief or the Help Everyone Belief, or to put it another way, compulsive helpers.

> I had really painful abdominal cramps and was feeling feverish, but I had to do a theatre list: a general anaesthetic list for children. Some had waited six months or more, with very decaying teeth, needing extractions. This takes a whole team: a dentist, consultant anaesthetist, dental nurse, people on the ward, so if you cancel that's a huge loss. I thought to myself, I am the only one who can do this and if I don't do it they'll all have to go back on a waiting list. In my mind being Miss make-the-most-of-time, I thought, I'll kill two birds with one stone. I'll be in a hospital anyway; I'll get myself checked out afterwards. I got through the hospital door and collapsed. I remember seeing faces above me thinking what's going on. I had to have a major operation and was off work for three months. And the list still got done by another dentist. Yet I'd convinced myself that I could save the day and deal with my own needs afterwards. I remember lying there in the hospital bed when I heard that the children got seen to, thinking to myself, You're such an idiot! Those kids were fine. You put your own life at risk.
>
> Dentist, Interviewee

I've already defined the Super-Helper Syndrome as compulsive helping coupled with denial of one's own needs. Those who do deny their own needs can sometimes achieve a degree of gratification by outsourcing the need to be cared for to someone else. Some even unconsciously seek out these relationships. It's a psychoanalytical defence mechanism known as 'reversal'. The eminent psychoanalyst Nancy McWilliams explains it like this: 'If one feels that the yearning to be cared for by someone else is shameful or dangerous, one can vicariously satisfy one's own dependency needs by taking care of another person.'

145

The need to be needed makes people vulnerable to the They-Couldn't-Survive-Without-Me Belief. One of my favourite films, some distance behind *Sleepless*, is Zoe Kazan's romantic comedy, *Ruby Sparks*. It's about a writer, Calvin, who conjures up his ideal girlfriend. But when Ruby turns out to be a self-determined woman, he rewrites her character as miserable without him. After that she becomes so clingy that when he accidentally separates from her at a pedestrian crossing, she is left crying on the sidewalk. My favourite line is when Ruby tearfully says, 'You let go of my hand.' If you haven't watched it ... spotlight homework for tonight!

Codependent Tendencies

One form of the CS relationship that has received a lot of attention is the idea of codependency. Lois Wilson was the wife of one of the founders of Alcoholics Anonymous (AA). She battled against her husband's addiction, dedicating her life to supporting him. In her memoir she wrote, 'I had faith in my own power to change him. Living with me would be such an inspiration, I thought, that he would not need the balm of alcohol.' She upped sticks and followed him around the US on a motorbike, hoping this lifestyle might curb his drinking. She even blamed herself, wondering if her repeated miscarriages spurred him back to drink. When he finally quit the booze, however, her life wasn't any better. Her husband swapped his drinking for activism in AA. She still followed him around, but now it was to AA meetings. She realised he didn't need her in the way he had before. Her whole aim in life, to help him achieve sobriety, had been deleted. 'Little by little I saw that my ego had been nourished during his drinking years by the important roles I had to fill: mother, nurse, breadwinner, decision maker.' Part of her had actually been glad that he drank. She needed it too. She had been the rescuer. In the end she set up Al-Anon, a support group for the families of alcoholics, helping them understand their own needs and the mistakes they make. Members started to call themselves co-alcoholics. Later, the broader term codependent was adopted.

The most powerful voice in relation to codependency has been Melody Beattie. She made it into a household term and has written a clutch of books on the subject. Although some have criticised her for being anecdotal or unscientific, and codependency is not a recognised psychological disorder, her wisdom clearly resonates with people. For example, when she says, 'You need to detach most when it seems the least likely or possible thing to do.' Beattie too had a history of drink and drugs, becoming an alcoholic at the age of 13, and later marrying a man who claimed to be a recovering alcoholic but who was still drinking in secret.

When she was working as a counsellor in a treatment centre, her employer told her to set up support groups for wives of the addicts. Initially she was scathing about these codependents, seeing them as hostile, controlling and manipulative. Over time, she got to know them better. Now that she was sober, she found that she too had become codependent, caught up in her relationships with the alcoholics in her own life. She went along to Al-Anon meetings:

> After floundering in despair for a while, I began to understand. Like many people who judge others harshly, I realised I had just taken a very long and painful walk in the shoes of those I had judged. I now understood those crazy codependents. I had become one.

It's a hard thing to face up to. One interviewee, a support worker for a charity working with vulnerable adults, told me how she had spent ten years in therapy to resolve her own traumatic past. In the end she saw that she couldn't fix her own childhood by trying to fix her clients. It's important for anyone in a CS relationship to honestly examine their own motives. To consider whether they have a propensity for this type of relationship and why, either in the form of reversal or codependency or to meet some other underlying psychological need of their own. Mapping this onto the criteria for the They-Couldn't-Survive-Without-Me Belief, the helper has to question whether they are truly indispensable.

Codependency was flagged up during my counselling sessions. I always looked for lame ducks who needed help. In a romantic partner if someone was too sorted and confident that would alienate me. I had some really good offers, but I'd turn them down for the guy who had anxiety or needed mothering.

Psychologist, Interviewee

Dependent Tendencies

It can be the other way round. Sometimes the characteristics of the dependent person bring about a CS relationship. Remember the example of my psychologist friend who spent months on the phone to a guy who kept on splitting up with his girlfriend. That guy, despite having a degree from one of the best universities, repeatedly positioned himself as incompetent in many aspects of his life. My friend spent hours counselling him and offering reassurance. He had quickly fallen into that role. All they ever talked about was the other man's insecurities: either his career worries which continued after he landed a prestigious new job; his relationship with his previous partner; or the women he started dating. My friend confessed to me how conflicted he was: he wanted to help and hated feeling resentful. When he started to limit his help they drifted apart. The guy attached himself to a procession of other rescuers. It took a long time for my friend to get over his sense of loss of the relationship, despite it always being imbalanced.

My friend also told me that he wondered if the man had Dependent Personality Disorder (DPD). He hadn't carried out an assessment, as would be required for a formal diagnosis, but the man did seem to meet most of the criteria. The *Diagnostic and Statistical Manual of Mental Disorders* (*DSM V*) is the go-to reference for psychiatrists and clinical psychologists. Dependent Personality Disorder is defined as an excessive need to rely on others for support, guidance, nurturance and protection. DPD is characterised by high anxiety, which is triggered by making everyday decisions, even the simplest ones like what to eat or what to wear. People with DPD feel helpless on their own and vulnerable to rejection. Two sets of beliefs have been associated with it: a sense of personal ineffectiveness, and a view of the world as dangerous. To reduce their distress they turn to others. They might not ask for help directly, but might express their anxieties. This gets the compulsive helper's empathy radar bleeping.

Compulsive helpers can be a magnet for people with dependent tendencies, and vice versa. For that reason, you need to make a conscious decision about whether to get involved. If you do start helping, you need to keep a close eye on the amount of help you give. There's also a risk of reinforcing the dependent person's inability to cope on their own. In fact, people with DPD can get stuck: they fear that becoming more independent increases the risk of abandonment. Here, the helper could challenge themselves by reflecting on the second criterion for the They-Couldn't-Survive-Without-Me Belief – total dependency. Would the person collapse or die without your help?

There were other examples of CS relationships involving personality disorders in the data I collected. These represented extreme challenges for those who were trying to help them. Here are the words of one mother who told me about caring for her daughter:

She started self-harming when she was about 15. She's covered in scars. She covers the scars in tattoos. She would just rage; you'd think here's a hysterical mad woman, some psycho! It's quite frightening to deal with. I was the only one who could calm her down. The BPD voice went round her head telling her she was worthless. She believed the only person who loved her was me. She says that the only reason she didn't kill herself was me. I felt guilty because I hadn't done more earlier. If I asked her, she would just lie and pretend everything was fine. She calls me first thing in the morning, several times throughout the day, and every evening. She would call me and I'd drop everything and drive forty-five minutes to her. If she was in that frame of mind, she'd self-harm anyway. I might have prevented her from doing it more, but usually she'd already cut herself. My feeling of utter helplessness. I still have to be on call. I'm still her lifeline. My current husband has been a rock; he knows I have to pick up the phone, drive off at the drop of a hat. What worries me is what happens when I'm not here? What happens when I start to get frail?

Borderline Personality Disorder (BPD) is sometimes also referred to as Emotionally Unstable Personality Disorder. It's a broad term and complex to diagnose. According to the *DSM V*, those with BPD find it difficult to maintain stable relationships. They experience impulsive behaviours such as binge eating and drug or alcohol abuse. They're also prone to self-harm and suicidal feelings. From the point of view of someone trying to care for them, they can be highly dependent but can also turn against the helper, expressing extreme anger or claiming that they aren't really loved. Because of their clinging behaviour and threats to take their own life they can reinforce the helper's belief that They Couldn't Survive Without Me.

Narcissistic Personality Disorder – Forsaken Sons and Dutiful Daughters

I also interviewed several helpers who talked about CS relationships with someone who they believed had Narcissistic Personality Disorder (NPD). It's a fashionable term these days. There are frequent accusations of narcissism aimed at celebrities and politicians, which may or may not be accurate. A classic example would be Shakespeare's King Lear, whose need for attention and lack of empathy goes so far as to ask his daughters to declare which of them loves him the most. But the *DSM V* provides a clear set of criteria for its clinical diagnosis. People with NPD have a grandiose sense of self-importance. They have fantasies of success and power or ideal love. Whatever their position in life, they believe that they are special and should associate with people of high status. They believe that others are envious of them. They typically see themselves as fascinating and beautiful and pay a lot of attention to what they wear, setting out to impress. This can make them initially attractive or interesting to strangers. They can be flirtatious and seductive, drawing people into their orbit. But their relationships are marred by a sense of entitlement. They exploit their family and friends, picking up and dropping people.

I've already introduced you to my own mother. When I was a child my whole life was about reading and anticipating her moods and meeting her needs. Her world had to be exactly the way she wanted, from the position of the ceramic Whimsies on the windowsill to the level of milk left in the bottle.

If people came to the house, I was forced to play the piano for them. She dressed me up in make-up and sent me to dance school from the age of 4. She made me audition for the role of Gretl in the *Sound of Music* when it came to the London stage with Petula Clark. We queued in the rain outside the Apollo Victoria before I got to sing and dance. We were called back through various stages of auditions and interviewed in the famously long queue by BBC News. My mother couldn't have been happier. I eventually made it down to the last few contenders. When they called the next candidate, my mother yelled out from the gods, 'Give her another chance!'

She would dress me in the same clothes as her. There's a photo of us in matching pink minidresses, doing a showgirl pose. She carted me around like a trophy, paraded me before the ladies at church. If anyone called me pretty, my mother would say, 'Not as pretty as me' or 'But she's not attractive'. She'd had some topless photos done, and tried to become a glamour model, and wanted this for me too. To improve my chances, when she had a facelift, she asked about the cost of breast implants for me. The surgeon said I was too young.

As well as a fixation on how I looked, she believed herself to be irresistible. She would prance around the house naked. My father went AWOL as soon as I was conceived, but for many years she clung onto the fantasy that he loved her. She flirted with her friends' husbands in front of them, yet I wasn't allowed to play with their children: they weren't good enough. Two of the churches we joined banned her for disruptive behaviour, either rude or flirtatious.

Whenever I got a job, she would take my first pay packet, saying I owed it to her. She had me. She brought me up. What had I done for her?

There was another mother and daughter who lived locally and were always together. They walked arm-in-arm as the daughter moved through her 30s and 40s. My mother would point to them and say, 'That's how we're going to be.' She made it clear that she couldn't survive without me, and that it was my duty to ensure that she did survive.

For much of my life I looked after her. Later on, whenever she was ill or taken into hospital, I'd stop what I was doing and race back. Even today I ask myself if I could have done more to help her. I question myself about whether I am making a fuss about nothing. That's something I've heard from other children of narcissistic parents. Again, no one calls it out: they say, 'I'm sure your mother loved you; she was only doing her best. You are her daughter, so you should care for her.'

Antisocial Personality Disorder – When Helpers Get Used

When someone deliberately takes advantage of someone else's compassion, that is straightforward exploitation. The exploiter is the rafflesia, living parasitically. I never looked after my father in the way I looked after my mother, but he attracted and made use of plenty of other helpers. He met all the diagnostic requirements for Antisocial Personality Disorder (ASPD).

About half the men in prison have ASPD. My father never went to prison. He told me only stupid people get caught. People with this disorder have no scruples about acting unlawfully. Lying comes easily to them and they readily con people for profit or pleasure. Their dishonesty and unreliability are exhibited in a failure to sustain work commitments or to honour financial obligations. They can also be violent. They display a reckless disregard for themselves and for others, and act without responsibility. In the face of all these antisocial acts they lack remorse or a sense of guilt.

> At times I locked myself in the bathroom so he couldn't get to me. When I came out he'd pick me up and carry me. He'd take me into the street, smash a bottle and threaten me with it. I was his property, wasn't I, so I had to do what he said. In those days there was no coercive control or rape in a marriage. I couldn't tell anyone. I was 25 and had two children to take care of. And who could I phone? He was in the police force. I bumped into his friend, who said, 'I thought he'd buried you in the garden.'
>
> Interviewee

My father told me to look after number one. His creed included the advice that you can't trust anyone. He joined the army at 16. In the Second World

War he fought his way across Africa and up through Italy. He was in small groups of soldiers and sometimes behind enemy lines. He took part in a number of major battles that he never talked about. Some acts that in times of peace would get you sent to prison, in times of war get you a medal.

My father had a reputation for reckless bravery. He searched out and rescued a soldier who had stepped on a mine and he was commended by a senior officer. When I was in secondary school, he told me that one of the men in his battalion had been stealing battle keepsakes from his comrades. One day the soldier turned his back to have a piss. My father shot him.

After the war he ran a betting shop. He boasted to me about hanging out with 'Mad' Frankie Fraser, the gangster who turned to crime at the age of 10 and spent forty-two years in prison. Mad Frankie also spent time in and out of mental hospitals. He was part of the Richardson Gang, notorious for burning and electrocuting those who were disloyal. Mad Frankie was accused of pulling out his victims' teeth with a pair of pliers. He went on to write an autobiography and to appear on stage, television and in films. My father went on to be a financial adviser.

He also went on to have many lovers, and a squad of children. He attracted women the way a black hole destroys stars, and they cared for his needs. They were prepared to do anything to hold onto the belief that he loved them. He was married to another woman when he met my mother, and he never lived with us. When he was supposed to come and visit me, I waited beside the window all dressed up. He seldom came. When he did, he would stare at me while I was watching television. Then he would say, 'You blink a lot, don't you?'

Once, when he had been kicked out by another of his women, he slept in his car outside our house so my mother would take him in. I was about 12 at the time and he agreed to drive me to school that morning. A motorcycle cut across in front of us in the heavy London traffic, so my father pulled on the handbrake and got out. He went up to the motorcyclist and told him to get off his bike. He barked at the man several times to take off his helmet. Then my father punched him right in the face.

As a financial adviser on commission, he sold my mother a policy that she paid into for more than thirty years. It was supposed to provide her with a benefit of £6,000 at the time of his death. When I stopped the payments, she had put in more than £17,000. He outlived her by eight months. Mad Frankie died at age 90. My father, also called Frank, went on to 93. There's a certain type of man who is practically indestructible.

You might think that it's obvious you don't want to end up in a helping relationship with a psychopath. But people with ASPD are skilled at enticing others into their web. Like narcissists, they are often charming and good at flattery. They may not have any compassion when it comes to caring about how other people are feeling, but they can have scary quantities of cognitive empathy. They know exactly how to manipulate people. For years I was in thrall to my father, idolising him even when he didn't show up. I wasn't the only one.

Psychopaths exhibit power and strength and use these to trap people who might be of use to them.

> I started cleaning other people's houses secretly [laughs awkwardly] when he was at work and the children were at school because I just didn't have any money at all. I needed to start saving so that I could leave him.
>
> Nurse, Interviewee

When it comes to a life partner, someone with ASPD wants a servant or a slave. Sometimes they withhold money from those who care for them in order to retain all the power. A helper who asks for little in return is perfect. Some of the most extreme cases of Super-Helper Syndrome are when a natural helper believes someone with ASPD needs them, couldn't survive without them. They are right. They are needed. The way rafflesia needs other plants to feed off.

The Duty of Care

Psychological disorders aren't stereotypical. There are many forms of suffering. As well as those described above, there is a panoply of personality disorders, from avoidant, to histrionic, to depressive. Sometimes they are misdiagnosed; sometimes they go undiagnosed. All of them have their particular challenges and they often come with associated comorbidities; my mother had learning disabilities and anxiety disorders to compound her problems. Often they result from early trauma and often they contain hereditary elements. Neither of these is the fault of the person with the disorder. They do need help, but they need professional help in addition to the care they get from family and friends. It takes the right combination of therapies and expertise. But there are treatments. A partner, friend or family member in a CS relationship with a dependant who needs professional help will not be able to rescue that person, no matter how hard they try.

Many find themselves caring for those who require intensive attention and who are unable to give a great deal in return, whether it's for mental health or physical disability reasons or because the dependant is too young or too old to look after themselves. Any type of CS relationship can lead to the Super-Helper Syndrome: exhaustion, resentment, exploitation and self-criticism. And other difficulties: those who care for a dependant often feel alone. Their own needs are quickly forgotten. As I mentioned earlier, this can feel like part of the duty of care. There can be serious financial worries. For some, full-time caring makes it difficult to find employment. If they did get a job it wouldn't be enough to cover the cost of care. So many helpers said their hands were tied, they had no control, no power. At this point I want to write several pages reporting back the pain I could almost touch; their frustration at not being able to get the support they or their dependants needed; the hours filling in forms or on the phone to health and social services; ending up on long waiting lists or being told their situation is not bad enough to warrant attention.

I wish I could do something about all that. As a coach, all I can do is listen to them and try to understand their situation. All I can do is remind them that there are things that they can influence and that those things are mostly to do with their own thinking. That's what I want to do here.

Whatever type of CS relationship you're in – whether the dependant is a relative, partner, a boss, colleagues, customers or patients, or anyone else – it's easy to feel stuck. And that feeling is reinforced when you believe you are indispensable, when you believe someone is totally dependent on you, and when you feel you have no choice. That's why it's so important to see that the They-Couldn't-Survive-Without-Me Belief is irrational. This belief narrows your horizons and blinds you from the choices you have. It stops you from even looking for solutions.

Deconstructing the They-Couldn't-Survive-Without-Me Belief

Acknowledge You HOLD the Belief

If you hold this belief, it's axiomatic to how you live. To you, it is obviously true. You would never question it. But the belief is likely to be unconscious. The first stage is to bring it out into the light of day and acknowledge it.

EXPOSE the Belief as Irrational

This is a tough part. I'm frantically waving the red flag in case there's still a wall of resistance.

In practical terms the belief appears to be true. If you are caring for someone who can't feed, dress or take themselves to the toilet, you might have strong words for anyone who comes along and says your belief that they couldn't survive without you is irrational.

To expose the belief as irrational you have to refute at least one of the defining criteria: that you are indispensable, that there is total dependency and that you have no choice.

1. You are dispensable. While you feel indispensable, in reality, this is not the case. Because it can be difficult to see, here's a logical argument to look at whether the helper is really indispensable. Try the following thought experiment.

Spotlight 7.1: *Are You Indispensable?*

June looks after David who has dementia. June believes she is indispensable and that nobody else has the capability and the availability to provide the care David needs.

Next door, Mary looks after Bert who has dementia. Mary believes she is indispensable and that nobody else has the capability and the availability to provide the care Bert needs.

One day they decide to swap. Now June looks after Bert and Mary looks after David.

What happens next?

For helpers in some types of CS relationships, it can be useful to remember that there are other people out there just like your dependant. You aren't looking after those people. They survive without you. Just like June and Mary, this illustrates that you really aren't indispensable.

If you believe that there's nobody else with the capability and the availability to provide the care your dependant needs, or your dependant won't accept help from anyone else, imagine the following.

Spotlight 7.2: *Alien Abduction (Part 1)*

Two giant silver round metal ravioli land in your street. The top half of the nearest craft pivots open with an impressive mechanical whirr. From it, three small blue aliens float into your home. They abduct you in the gentlest and most courteous manner, insisting that you come and live on their planet. They say that you've been specially selected and only you are allowed to come.

As they escort you to their waiting spacecraft, the alien team leader explains that his colleagues in the other ship will arrange a thorough care plan including anything that you wish to put in place for your dependant.

What happens next?

2. They are not totally dependent. Although it's never true that you are indispensable, it can be the case that someone is totally dependent. In Spotlight 7.1 above, David and Bert did need care. But as we've seen, this is not true for all CS relationships. Sometimes the helpee is not totally dependent. If they didn't receive their current level of help, there wouldn't be extreme consequences: they wouldn't collapse or die. Think about the story of the cobbler. Think about the colleagues of someone who doesn't dare to take time off work. Think about the examples of codependency where the relationship is actually harmful to both people.

3. You do have a choice. There are always other options, even if you are currently unable to see them. Everyone thinks they are the exception – in my unique circumstances I have no option. But if you let go of the They-Couldn't-Survive-Without-Me Belief it doesn't imply that you are going to abandon your dependant altogether. That's another irrational thought. Letting go of the belief doesn't mean you love them any less. It doesn't have to be all or nothing, total self-sacrifice or total abandonment. That's what the belief wants you to think. Possibly what your dependant wants you to think. Just knowing you have choices can be hugely liberating, even if you then choose to do exactly as you have done before. At least it's your choice.

If you are finding it hard to accept that you have choices, try this thought experiment.

Spotlight 7.3: *Imagine Your Choices*

Imagine you have a friend who is exactly like you: same face, height, hairstyle and the same personality. They live in a home that looks exactly like the one you live in. Everything about their life looks exactly the same as yours, including the person or people they are caring for. They feel exactly the way you do.

What would you tell this friend?

If you've drawn a blank on this, you might like to imagine that the friend is sitting in a chair opposite you. You could try suggesting what they could do. You could work through the four forms of help: what resources, information, expert or supportive help does your imaginary friend need?

If you are still having trouble imagining that you have any choice, you might want to look at *Choice Theory* by William Glasser. He was a leading psychiatrist who called attention to how we choose all our behaviour. His work is especially relevant to this chapter because he saw good relationships as one of the keys to a successful life. Following in the footsteps of people like Alfred Adler, he believed that all long-lasting psychological problems are relationship problems. According to Glasser, 'Whenever you feel as if you don't have the freedom you want in a relationship, it is because you, your partner, or both of you are unwilling to accept the choice theory axiom: *You can only control your own life.*'

EXPOSE the Belief as Harmful

The harms that come from this belief are manifold. I've already mentioned how it can leave the helper feeling exhausted, isolated and unappreciated. If you are in an unhealthy relationship looking after someone else, you can get to age 40 (or 50 or 60) and realise, I don't have a life and I haven't had one for years. Resentment follows. You feel like a caged bird.

As we've seen when we talked about codependency, or people who need professional help that they are not getting, this belief may also be harmful to the dependant.

Spotlight 7.4: *What's the Harm?*

Write this down, or rant into a voice recorder app.

List all of the harmful effects of your CS relationship.
Express how you feel.
Don't hold back because nobody else is ever going to see or listen to it.

If you feel brave, read through your list or listen back to your recording. If you found it difficult to answer Spotlight 7.3 you might like to try it again now.

Now that you've purged using Spotlight 7.4, it's time to ...

LET GO of the Belief

Even if you accept in principle all the arguments above for refuting the belief, it is difficult to let go of it. Even when the birdcage is already open.

It can be painful to realise that you have been living someone else's story, not your own. You are a minor character in your own life, the deuteragonist in someone else's. It's understandable to feel a sense of loss.

Letting go of the belief can sometimes mean letting go of a sense of self-importance. There can be some gratification in playing the part of the martyr, for example as the matriarch of the family, or the ideal son or daughter. The idea that you are indispensable is part of your identity. There is an element of helper's pride in looking after a dependant or sacrificing yourself for your team. Your belief that you are indispensable at work can give you a sense that you are valued and that your job is secure. It can also be an excuse for holding yourself back in your career (that's one way to interpret the ending of the story of the boy and the cobbler).

The CS relationship takes two. The other person may need to let go of their I-Couldn't-Survive-Without-You belief too. You don't have control over that. You can only take control of your own thoughts. You have to let go of the belief even if they don't.

If you have been caring for someone with a disorder that leaves them with little or no empathy you have to let go of the sadness that they cannot love you back. You have to let go of the part of yourself you have given to the relationship, maybe for many years. You have to let go of the hope that your relationship could ever be different.

PUT Something in its Place

An alternative rational belief is 'I know and respect the limits of my responsibility to help'. What you do next is contingent on your circumstances. You might continue to look after your dependant in much the same way, but with a renewed sense that it's your conscious choice to do so. You might continue to support your dependant but in a reduced role rather than them being totally dependent on you. If so, you will need a plan and support mechanisms, both for you and for your dependant. Remember, reducing your capacity as the helper doesn't mean reducing your love.

It might be right for you to end the CS relationship altogether. If you are in an abusive or exploitative relationship, ideally, you just walk away. It is not your responsibility to help. But it's seldom as simple as this and comes with a host of complications. There's a continuum of possibilities for your future relationship, everything from managing your level of responsibility within defined boundaries all the way through to zero contact. Again, you will need a plan and support mechanisms.

Your first and most important task is to have the courage to ask for help yourself. And the place to start is with the people who love you. Or anyone who has been through something similar and can advise you. The next task is to find out what other resources and support are available. Because the challenges of CS relationships are widely recognised, there are numerous groups and organisations covering a range of specific situations. These include charities, helplines, community support services and online forums, in addition to healthcare resources.

Another crucial skill to stop you sliding back into an old CS relationship, or to stop you from falling into a new one, is learning to set boundaries. That's how you protect your own needs. I'll get to boundaries soon. But you can't protect your needs if you don't know what they are. That's what the next two chapters are all about.

Chapter 8

The No Needs Belief

We have now completed our tour of the three irrational beliefs that underlie compulsive helping. In terms of the little formula (CH × NN = SHS) we are halfway there. The Super-Helper Syndrome is a combination of the compulsion to help AND not meeting your own needs. Compulsive helping alone is no crime. The real trouble comes from neglecting your own needs. And, let's be honest, if you are compulsively helping others you are highly unlikely to be paying much attention to yourself. Just before the formula there was a spotlight (3.2) about how well you are meeting your needs. They were grouped into eleven categories. Now would be a good time to review that, or to complete it if you haven't already. Don't be alarmed if your self-scoring is low for most, or even all, of the categories. That's what happens when my clients complete it.

Because helpers resist the idea of meeting their own needs, this chapter comes with an amber warning flag for ambivalence. When I introduced you to the formula, I also mentioned that helpers take pride in not meeting their own needs. My interviewees would smile and say they know that they should look after themselves more, but I was left doubting whether they would do anything about it. This idea of pride emerged in many of the interviews and, on reflection, it's been the backdrop to my conversations with helpers over the years. Helper's pride is the flip side of helper's guilt. Pride in not meeting your own needs, and guilt for not helping enough. Both of these are warped. It's as if helpers get a thrill from surviving on the edge of collapse. They are like the person who dashes across a busy street, dodging the cars, to catch a bus. Even as they do it, they know they are taking an unnecessary risk. But as they come to land in their seat they feel more alive. Their heart pounds and their breath rushes; they got away with it. They wrap themselves in a hero's cape, telling themselves they are indestructible. But they are destructible; secretly, they know this.

Compulsive helping without looking after your own needs is not sustainable. There wasn't a single helper who I heard from who hadn't struggled at some point or other to meet their own needs. Shattered nurses dared not take annual leave because their colleagues were overstretched too. There was no one to take their place. A manager of care homes worried about his staff: many were workaholics, staying late after their shift, when they were already in tatters. A charity worker did the 5 a.m. outreach as well as twelve-hour shifts in homeless hostels for over a year before she realised how tired she was. A care worker didn't have time 'to sleep, eat, digest, pee, read, go for a walk. Little things!' The list goes on.

It's not only professional carers who struggle to look after their own needs. Few people find it easy; that's why so many of us eat or drink too much, delay booking that dental appointment or don't take the exercise we know would be good for us. Those are obvious and basic needs, but the neglect climbs the whole tree. Even when they are meeting their basic needs, helpers fail to meet their higher order needs: categories like Psychological, Aspirational and Soul needs (as in the list in Spotlight 3.2).

Some don't have a primary relationship. They stare at an empty ring finger but they aren't doing anything about it. Or where they are, they sabotage their efforts. Ironically, one of the examples of this was a family lawyer who spent her working life advising on other people's divorces. In her 'spare' time she sorted out her friends' problems. There was no room in her diary for romance. Others, who do have a partner, still don't consider their own needs within that relationship. One client repeatedly asked her husband if he was happy with the life they had together – was it what he had in mind?

Excuses, Excuses

Helpers commonly say that they are too busy to look after themselves. They say they have to focus on the needs of others. And for some, that is true. Many professional carers are in situations where it is difficult to pay much attention to their own needs. But fundamentally those are excuses and signs of another irrational belief. Secretly thinking it's selfish to meet your own needs is a shibboleth that you hold the No Needs Belief. This is the fourth irrational belief that underlies the Super-Helper Syndrome: 'I *shouldn't* have any needs.' It is possibly the most insidious of the four because it's an excuse itself. An excuse for wading into the riptide.

Spotlight 8.1: *What's Your Story?*

When was the last time you used one of these excuses to avoid meeting your own needs?

'Oh me? I'm fine.'
'I'm too busy.'
'But they really need me right now.'
'It feels selfish to focus on me.'
'Helping is just what I do; I'll get through somehow.'

What other creative excuses do you use?

It's only when you admit that these are excuses that you have any real possibility of letting go of the No Needs Belief when we come to deconstructing it.

Like the other shoulds and musts, the No Needs Belief is unconscious. People don't go around saying to themselves, 'I shouldn't have any needs.' The belief shows up in excuses. It shows up in the choices we make. It shows up in our priorities.

The Silent Woman

When my client above told me how she asked her husband if he was happy in their relationship, I was shocked. I wanted to say, 'Where are you in your relationship?' 'What about your rights? Did your husband turn round and ask if you are happy? Does responsibility for the health of the relationship rest solely on your shoulders?' My client had completely filtered out her own needs. And she was in a loving relationship with a sensitive and supportive man. Having needs was not a room she ever entered. She's not the only one.

Rod's mother was a woman who never expressed her own needs. She devoted her life to looking after her family and many others. She joined a community whose main ethos was about taking in people in need: those recovering from addictions or domestic abuse. She was unseen, out the back chopping onions for large communal meals. Later in life she did voluntary work in the Middle East.

We visited her at home shortly before she went back into hospital during her last illness. She was frail and thin. In the sitting room, there was a conflab going on about whether she was well enough for us to take her for a pub lunch. The discussion continued as she slipped out of the room and came back. By then, her husband had ruled that it would be better for her not to go. She had placed her little sheepskin boots discreetly beside her chair. It looked like a signal that she did want to go, so I felt I had to point that out. That lunch was the last time we ever went out to eat together. I remember the pub was called The Silent Woman.

Spotting Your Blind Spot

When someone doesn't even know what their needs are, that in itself is forensic evidence they hold the No Needs Belief. Thinking about what they want isn't part of their internal lexicon. The only need they can identify is their need to help others. And, by the way, that doesn't count!

When confronted with this, it is easy to think, 'But I do know what my needs are!' I need a coffee first thing in the morning and I know which mug

I like to drink it from. I know *Sleepless* is my favourite movie. But these are tastes and preferences that don't affect anyone else. Someone who holds the No Needs Belief doesn't have needs that affect anyone else. Whenever there's an intersection with the possible needs of another person, theirs give way. They accommodate what the other person wants and then rationalise this. For example, her partner says, 'I don't fancy going out tonight,' and she says, 'Great, we can finish off the pizza in the fridge.' It doesn't even occur to her to consider what she wants to do. She doesn't see the total eclipse of her needs.

Previously I mentioned how some helpers become the fixer in the family, the one who everyone else turns to. For some of the men I interviewed this meant falling into the role of mediator. He's the go-between when his siblings or parents have disputes. He's the peacekeeper at work or among his friends. He patiently listens as each of them come to him with their views about the situation. They trust him to remain neutral, to hold what they say in confidence, and put his own needs aside. All this leaves him exhausted: 'It's flipping hard work sometimes.'

Spotlight 8.2: *Putting Your Blind Spot in the Spotlight*

If you suspect you might have a blind spot for your own needs you could do a little ethnological field research. Over the next week or so, whenever you are with others, observe how frequently they express their needs and how often you do. Are you expressing a need or is it just a preference? What happens when there's an intersection of needs? Who accommodates the other? Who gets their own way?

When someone is in the habit of accommodating others' needs, they can be blinkered from seeing that that's what they do. It's subtle. They are not aware of what they aren't aware of. Everyone around them is likely to be content with the status quo. It's unlikely they notice and, if they do, they have no motive to draw attention to it. They benefit from expressing their own needs without anything getting in their way. The people I interviewed feared being seen as pathetic, a pushover, a people-pleaser, a doormat. They knew they were being taken for granted – the exploitation of the Super-Helper Syndrome. They only become aware of the No Needs Belief when it is pointed out by a trusted friend or a coach. And when that happens there are two stock responses I hear:

1. 'I'm just a nice person.' (Using the Good Person Belief as an excuse.)
2. 'I suppose I'm just the sort of person who doesn't seem to have any needs.' (Excuses, watery excuses.)

When I was discussing all this with a psychologist friend, she protested that she did express her needs. She had been hounding her husband for months about plans for a particular weekend. When I asked what the weekend was, she said she wanted to host a special gathering for his 40th birthday. (Hoisted by her own NNB!) Just to be really clear, that is an example of the need to help others. It still doesn't count! Use the spotlight below if you want to identify the degree to which you typically express your needs.

Spotlight 8.3: *Plans for the Weekend*

You've just looked up the weather forecast for the coming weekend. It is going to be gloriously warm and sunny at your favourite coastal spot. Which of the following would you be most likely to say to your partner (or friend or housemate)?

1. You don't say anything. You wait to see what they suggest.
2. 'What do you want to do at the weekend?'
3. 'What shall we do this weekend?'
4. 'How do you feel about going to the coast this weekend?'
5. 'Shall we go to the coast this weekend?'
6. 'I'd like to go to the coast this weekend.'
7. 'Let's go to the coast this weekend!'
8. 'I'm heading for the coast this weekend. Do you want to come?'

If you have a needs blind spot you might not even connect the expectation that it is going to be gloriously warm and sunny with your own desire to go to the coast. You'd pick option one above, with no agenda of your own. Other devotees of the No Needs Belief are unlikely to get beyond the first three options. You'd only use the fourth question if you had already discerned that it's what they would want (having activated your overdriven empathy circuit). But the other options are legitimate expressions of need. You can practise as the opportunity arises, adapting them to different situations, trying to see how far down the list you can get. It can be revealing how your partner or friend reacts when you start to use increasing degrees of expressing your needs. Also, listen out for the phrases other people use to express what they want to do.

If the last question in Spotlight 8.3 seems too rude for you ever to use, how does it sound when someone else says it? Would you immediately accommodate their needs? If you always ask them what they want, do they ever turn the question back to you, and ask what you'd prefer? Or do they simply go, *ker-ching!* and launch into expressing their needs.

Childhood Messages – Don't be Selfish!

The childhood messages that set up this belief are part of the same story as those that lead to the Good Person Belief. Take the little girl in Chapter 5 who was brought up to believe she must be helpful to be good. She's also likely to be told she shouldn't be selfish. As babies, we readily and instinctively express our needs. We are unable to do anything for ourselves, so we scream for attention. Adults accept this behaviour. But as a baby grows up, learns to talk and develops some capacity to look after itself, they can start to close down the expression of its needs. If a child is continually told that they are too demanding, gradually their own needs can be erased.

Esther Summerson in *Bleak House* comes to mind. Her aunt, who brought her up, told her, 'Your mother, Esther, is your disgrace, and you were hers.'

Her mother had had a love affair before her marriage, and Esther was the result. She was told, 'Submission, self-denial, diligent work, are the preparations for a life begun with such a shadow on it.' And so Esther sinks into Super-Helper Syndrome, never expressing her own needs and helping many people throughout the novel, to the point where this results in her becoming disfigured with smallpox. She agrees to marry John Jarndyce, a good man, but much older than her, and not the man she is in love with. Talking to her doll after hearing those childhood messages from her aunt, she says:

> I would try, as hard as ever I could, to repair the fault I had been born with (of which I confusedly felt guilty and yet innocent), and would strive as I grew up to be industrious, contented, and kind-hearted, and to do some good to someone, and win some love to myself if I could.

This last quote illustrates her Good Person Belief too.

A child can also develop the No Needs Belief if they have to look after their own parents – a role reversal known as the parentified child. The child can feel responsible for making a depressed parent better. When they fail at this, they too feel helpless and that they are to blame. According to the developmental psychologist Carolyn Zahn-Waxler, this can block personal growth and the formation of an autonomous identity, 'This inability to develop a "true self" is seen as a precursor to depression.'

Some of those I spoke to had to learn to anticipate the mood swings of a volatile parent. Some were closely monitored and edited by a critical parent. As a result, they were always on the alert for censure or threat, doing whatever they could to mitigate it.

> My mum had an abusive upbringing, substance abuse, suicide attempts, dysfunctional relationships. She was horizontal a lot of the time so you'd be creeping about because she'd be asleep or crying somewhere. When I was 5 the teacher was being hard on me and I was picked on. But I remember thinking I can't tell mum because she'll get stressed. One time the cat pooed in my bedroom and I couldn't tell her; it would have set her off. Right from my earliest memories she was always someone to be protected, supported and worried about. Age 6 she would send me to

the local shops. I knew that's what I had to do, that sort of carer feeling, you know?

Psychologist, Interviewee

One of the support workers I interviewed told me her parents were unable to attune to their children. They were neglected emotionally and physically. Things like not being washed and only having her hair brushed when her grandmother visited. They were taken out of school but not home-schooled. She was given no chance to individuate or build her own relationships, 'It was my job to regulate mum and dad's feelings. They relied on me to cheer them up.'

As adults these people still prioritise others by default. It can take as many years to develop a sense of their own needs as it did to learn to suppress them in the first place. Some never get there.

At the end of her life, when Rod's mother was lying in the hospice, her husband and sons were sitting around her bed. She hadn't spoken for days and had hardly moved. She was dosed up on morphine and they weren't even sure if she was conscious. She lurched forwards, half sat up in her bed and opened her eyes. She made a shooing motion with the backs of her hands. 'Off you go. Go on!' she said. Then slumped back down. Her bewildered family stared at each other in turn. After a brief conference across the bed about what to do, they reluctantly left her. Back in the family home, they discussed whether she had decided to die that night. In fact, she died a few days later when they were all at her bedside. Even in the last days of her cancer she was still taking care of her family, giving them the night off.

People who have previously had a clear sight of their own needs can lose this over time or through circumstances. They can even lose sight of their sense of identity in this way. All-consuming work can have this effect. So can the accumulation of responsibilities such as having your own children or looking after elderly parents. I meet clients who say, 'I don't know who I am anymore.' They have acquired the No Needs Belief. I've also seen this with people who find themselves in a CS relationship. In the context of taking on a dependant, they no longer allow themselves to have any needs. The dependant can cultivate and reinforce the No Needs Belief with their own belief: you shouldn't have any needs.

In whatever way it comes about, whether you grew up with it or acquired it, and whether or not it's coupled with compulsive helping, the belief that 'I shouldn't have any needs' drains the life out of people.

Deconstructing the No Needs Belief

Acknowledge You HOLD the Belief

As I've mentioned, this belief can be hidden under multiple layers of excuses. This makes it hard to see. Or perhaps you do see it, but still resist admitting it to yourself. Are you making a virtue of not meeting your own needs? Helper's pride.

The proof lies in your behaviour. Do you express your needs? To what extent are you meeting them? Having read this chapter, and especially if you've completed the spotlights, it should be apparent to you by now if you hold the No Needs Belief. All you have to do is acknowledge that you hold it.

EXPOSE the Belief as Irrational

Once you acknowledge you hold this belief, it's obvious that it's irrational. It's like the Trump Tower – wrong on so many levels. Since all human beings have needs it's only reasonable to accept that you have them too.

People who hold the belief often think it would be selfish to have needs. But again, they don't apply the rule consistently. They don't think it is selfish for anyone else to have needs. And if that's true, it's irrational to believe 'I shouldn't have any needs'. Meeting your needs is a human right.

EXPOSE the Belief as Harmful

The harm is all the things you aren't doing for yourself. Combined with compulsive helping this belief leads to the Super-Helper Syndrome. It leads directly to exhaustion, resentment, exploitation and self-criticism.

An additional harmful effect can be under-achievement. In Chapter 4, I mentioned the unjustified self-criticism of people who are successful in their careers but don't feel it. But there are some who don't achieve their full potential. They neglect their own career development. Nobody else is bothered – people who don't stand up for what they want get overlooked.

People with this belief don't just ignore their needs. They ignore all signs of the damage it is doing to them. That's no way to live. If you hold the No Needs Belief it's time to let go of it before it is too late.

LET GO of the Belief

As soon as you do decide to look after your own needs you start groping around in the realisation that you don't know where they are. You find yourself in a recursive loop examining your own motives, wondering, is this really my need or something I ought to need. You second-guess your own thinking. Even when you have accepted the undeniable fact that it's an irrational belief, it still feels unnatural. This is perfectly normal. It's just another form of self-doubt – like a newly released track brought to you exclusively by CRITICAL FM. It takes practice to become aware of something you've previously ignored.

There's also the fear of overcorrecting. The ugly premonition is that you might become egocentric. That you might turn into one of those people who think the world revolves around them. The opposite of the No Needs Belief: the It's-All-About-Me Belief! Well, let me reassure you. There's no risk of that. It's hard enough to go from being unaware of your needs to a place where you do look after them. You are never going to reach the other extreme. It's the Full Moon Phobia again. The very fact you are afraid of this means it could never happen.

PUT Something in Its Place

An alternative, more constructive belief is 'I deserve to have my own needs met'.

Doesn't that sound reasonable? Doesn't that sound refreshing? It's true. It's simple enough to say. If only, by repeating it twenty times a day, you could make the world right again. Of course, you could try that, but changing your habits requires commitment to daily practice with proven tools, not just self-help exhortations like 'CHANGE YOUR LIFE TODAY!'

The next chapter provides those tools. The first step is to identify what your needs are. Here's a thought experiment to get you started.

Spotlight 8.4: *Alien Abduction (Part 2)*

The aliens who abducted you in Spotlight 7.2 successfully navigate inter-stellar space and bring you to their planet. From your window in the silver raviolo you see a sprawling city below. You can almost smell the billowing fumes of toxic waste. Through the clouds of pollution you can make out grey skyscrapers. Traffic jams of hovering vehicles swarm below. Your heart sinks as you contemplate your new home. (See, you do have needs!)

The spacecraft continues on over broad seas. Bright sunshine floods through your porthole. Eventually you set down on a tropical island. There are blue skies above and golden sands at your feet. There's a fresh spring and a lake. There's a forest with all your favourite exotic fruits hanging from the trees. Before he leaves, the alien team leader tells you this is your island. Nobody else is allowed to set foot on it. It's just for you. There will be a small boat that visits once a week. It's not allowed to take you home, but it can bring anything you need.

What do you need?

We've now pulled apart all four of the irrational beliefs. By way of celebration for how far we've come, and also a quick recap, here's a spotlight that simply states all of the alternative beliefs I've suggested to replace the irrational ones.

Spotlight 8.5: *Full Affirmation of the Alternative Beliefs*

If you can put your hand on your heart and honestly read all of these aloud, you are well on the way to avoiding Super-Helper Syndrome:

'My self-worth is not dependent on helping others.'
'I know and respect the limits of my capacity to help.'
'I know and respect the limits of my responsibility to help.'
'I deserve to have my own needs met.'

If it doesn't feel entirely authentic at first, keep revisiting the deconstruction section of each of the beliefs.

Part Three

The Healthy Helper

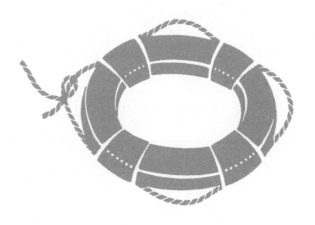

Chapter 9

The Healthy Helper Mindset

These days I look after myself as well as looking after my clients. I feel like I'm coming from a stronger place.

Therapist, Interviewee

In the last few chapters, we have ventured into some dank caves and shone a torch on each of the beliefs that give rise to compulsive helping. We've held a light to the damage done by not meeting your own needs. If you have been struggling with Super-Helper Syndrome and you've started work on countering those beliefs, then you deserve a Half Hug. It's only by exploring those places that you can come out the other side renewed. I know it can be tough work. You might be feeling regretful about the effects the beliefs have had on your life. You might be having doubts about who you are as a helper, or who you are as well as being a helper. You might be unsure about what comes next.

The good news is, now that we've dealt with all of the irrational beliefs, we've cleared the ground to open up a new possibility. I've been saying all along that I don't want to stop you helping. Now is the time to demonstrate that. Now's the time to remind ourselves of all the good things about helping. How, when it comes from compassion, it can bring joy, not just to the person being helped but to the helper as well. Now's the time to create a fresh mindset: the Healthy Helper Mindset.

Mindset interventions work by presenting you with the facts, providing examples of people who have adopted the new mindset, and by inviting you to write about how the new mindset can work for you. To start, come with me on a science walk through all the restorative benefits of helping.

Caring Calms You Down

We've all heard of the fight or flight responses to stress but more recently psychologists have unearthed another set of responses – 'tend and befriend'. In some stressful situations people turn towards others to give and receive support. This idea was first proposed because women sometimes react to stress in more healthy ways than men. The research suggests, in line with anecdotal evidence, that women are more prepared to talk through their stress with women friends, whereas men are more likely to bottle it up. This might be explained by the higher levels of oxytocin found in women. Oxytocin's effects are enhanced by the presence of oestrogen. From an evolutionary perspective the tend and befriend theory makes sense: ever since we first banded together in hunter-gatherer communities we've needed to stay close at times of danger, for safety and to tend to the young.

> As a mother, I've not pushed my girls to be 'helpful' or make them responsible for other people's emotions and happiness. It's something I've also learnt myself – to set a limit to my help and say when enough is enough.
>
> Teacher, Questionnaire Respondent

When we help, all the neurocircuitry of helping springs into action. As Kelly McGonigal, health psychologist at Stanford University puts it, 'When we care for others, it changes our biochemistry, activating systems of the brain that produce feelings of hope and courage.'

With this comes a plethora of benefits to the helper. In Chapter 6, I mentioned three systems within the brain that have been shown to be involved in prosocial behaviour. They were the attunement system, the social caregiving system and the reward circuits. In their review of the scientific evidence, Keltner and his colleagues pointed out that, 'emerging evidence suggests that acting with kindness yields many kinds of benefits for the giver'. The following paragraphs look at each of the three systems in turn.

Serotonin in the attunement system has been linked to helping because those with higher natural levels of this transmitter are more likely to act prosocially and less likely to act aggressively. Serotonin benefits the helper by more effective self-control and regulation of their emotions. It allows them to make better judgements about what to do in difficult circumstances.

Oxytocin in the social caregiving system of the brain helps to reduce anxiety. It can have a quiet word with the amygdala to calm it down when it's about to set off our fear response. So caring can actually make you feel braver. This reminds me of the stories in Christie Watson's inspiring nursing memoir, *The Courage to Care*. The neuroscience also suggests we can turn that around: caring gives you courage.

Third, the reward system of the brain makes us feel good about caring. Our neural slot machine pays out when we act generously, such as when we donate money. Dopamine also dampens our fear response and increases our desire to help. Keltner and his colleagues sum up: 'Collectively, these findings demonstrate the powerful role the dopamine-rich reward circuit of the brain plays in prosociality – in particular, by creating the "feeling good" effect of acting kindly.'

> I absolutely love helping others, especially if they're struggling and I can help them through a tough time. It's the knowing that I did something worthwhile to ease someone else's struggle a little.
>
> Gardener, Questionnaire Respondent

Helping Lifts You Up

Allan Luks is a leader of non-profit organisations, who has written extensively about the benefits of volunteering. In his surveys of thousands of volunteers across the US, many reported a boost to their self-worth, a positive side effect of knowing that they had made a difference. As one of my own questionnaire respondents put it, 'Helping makes me happy, gives me a sense of value and means that I actually like myself.'

Luks has found physical benefits too. In fact, 90 per cent of the volunteers said they experienced pleasant sensations such as physical warmth and increased energy. Some even felt euphoric. Luks refers to this as the 'Helper's High'. He claims it happens when the body experiences a rush of endorphins (natural opioids produced by the pituitary gland). After the initial high, more than half of the volunteers then felt calm and more optimistic about their own lives and, even, happier. It's the same pattern of sensations as the runner's high – one of the reasons people get hooked on exercise. Perhaps it's another reason helping too can become addictive.

As well as the feel-good factor and stress reduction, there's evidence of long-term health benefits. Luks' volunteers reported improvements in many conditions such as arthritis and asthma. Older people who suffered a bereavement and then took up volunteering lived longer than they might otherwise have expected. In his review of this type of research, public health expert Doug Oman reported that 'volunteering is associated on average with longer life, better self-rated health, and better physical functioning'.

As I was writing about the psychological benefits of help, just now, I took a coffee break and happened to hear a volunteer at a vaccination centre on the radio. She had been stewarding people in the queue outside when she was approached by a woman who was concerned about an elderly couple. They had struggled to get off a bus, the old man leaning heavily on his wife. Someone brought him a wheelchair. The woman wanted to leave cash for the couple to get a taxi home, so she gave it to the volunteer. She didn't want to draw attention to herself and didn't want the couple to know where the money came from. The volunteer went into the vaccination centre and found the couple. She asked them how they planned to get home. When they said by bus, she told them about the woman. As she handed over the money, both she and the elderly couple had tears in their eyes. She had phoned the radio station to make a public thank you because when she came back out, the woman had gone. This reminded me that just hearing stories of helping can uplift us. The benefits go beyond the helper and the person who is helped.

Caring Keeps You Connected

Remember the chimps who were grooming each other while we talked about reciprocity? They did this even when there was no immediate payback. The rewards were less transactional, and more geared towards maintaining social status as part of the group. It works for humans too. Earlier I mentioned Alfred Adler's separation of life tasks: the importance of identifying what is, and what is not, your responsibility. Another of his principles for human happiness was the notion of social interest, a sense of community and belonging. He called this *Gemeinschaftsgefühl* and it's a concept that is dear to me.

The scientist who led the research into tend and befriend responses to stress, Shelley Taylor, has also written a review paper on social support – the perception that you are loved and cared for by others. This sounds like an allied idea, one that continues Adler's thread. She looked at decades of research that point to the range of health and psychological benefits. For instance, supporting others cements personal relationships. It also makes it more likely that you receive help yourself when you need it. As Taylor mentions, even just believing this can be a comfort.

> I love helping others, particularly when I can see how the help has improved things for them and how much it meant to them. It's a lovely feeling to know I can do that for people I care about. I also think it deepens the relationship between us.
>
> Operations Manager, Questionnaire Respondent

We've now come to the end of our stroll through the science on the benefits of helping. The scientists who design mindset interventions use posters to sum up the evidence supporting the new mindset. Here's one for the Healthy Helper Mindset.

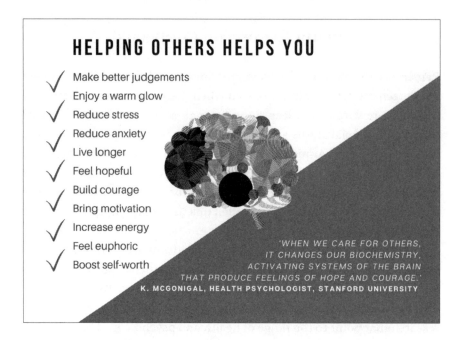

What Helping Means to Healthy Helpers

Mindset interventions use testimonials from people who have adopted the desired mindset. That's why I have peppered this chapter with quotes. Here's a few more responses from some of the healthy helpers when I asked, what does helping give to you?

> Helping others gives me a good feeling – it's my vocation.

> There's nothing more rewarding than knowing you've made a difference to someone's day, to someone's life; but I've learned that you can only help others if you are in a good place, so now I make sure I get the balance right.

> It makes my heart sing when they tell me how much I've helped them.

What Helping Means to You

Finally, rather than simply reading about it, mindset interventions ask people to write about how the new mindset can work for them. Doing this with the Healthy Helper Mindset can encourage you to commit to it and make it your own.

Spotlight 9.1: *What Healthy Helping Means to Me*

Having reviewed the scientific evidence and the testimonials of what helping means for others, now it's your turn. Write your own story of all the benefits that helping brings to you. Remember all the times when you've felt great about helping. Don't be afraid to be bold in claiming everything you have to gain.

This is the place to renew your relationship with helping. This is where you choose to be a healthy helper going forwards.

That's all the elements of the mindset intervention. If you've adopted the Healthy Helper Mindset, you will now be bristling with renewed excitement about your capacity to help. You know that not everyone has this gift. You know how helping deepens your connection with others. You know that helping benefits your health. Your brain and your body *are* wired to support you.

Meeting Your Needs

Armed with your shiny new Healthy Helper Mindset, it's time to talk again about your own needs. To be a healthy helper you have to look after these too. As I mentioned when we deconstructed the No Needs Belief, you can find yourself groping around with little idea of what your needs are. So, here's a list to choose from. I've revisited the eleven needs in Spotlight 3.2 so that you can reflect on each of them. They are broad headings and whole books have been written about them. I've just picked out a few suggestions that are particularly relevant for the survival of helpers.

Health – Cycles of Life

If all your attention has been on caring for others, it's easy to fall behind with medical and dental check-ups or to ignore symptoms. Neglecting your own health is a sign of the No Needs Belief. It's a matter of priority – you already know what to do to act in your own best interest.

Your body is designed to spend a third of its life asleep, but few people manage a good eight hours. A shortfall of sleep causes enough deleterious effects on the mind and body to keep anyone awake at night. For practical advice based on scientific research, I'd recommend *The Circadian Code* by Dr Satchin Panda. Reading that book a few years ago has noticeably improved my sleep. It also changed my relationship to light. Dr Panda taught me to activate my body's central clock at wake-up time. It's called the suprachiasmatic nucleus and it needs a good flood of brightness to kick it out of bed each morning. He also taught me to quieten the lights around the house in the evening. With the right quality of light, orange rather than blue, our bodies settle and prepare for sleep. A dark bedroom encourages the release of melatonin, the sleep hormone. Having spent a small fortune trying to black out the bedroom I've discovered a much cheaper and simpler solution: a silk eye mask.

Apart from anything else, Satchin Panda's book is a fascinating guide to the twenty-four-hour cycle of how the body digests food, repairs skin and gut lining, and detoxifies itself. But only if we allow it to go through its natural circadian rhythms. The most useful part for me has been the idea of stopping eating at least three hours before bed. Giving it enough time to rest allows the body to go into repair mode and produce growth hormone.

On the subject of hormones, I was interested to talk to Gabrielle Lichterman, founder of Hormonology. She told me that in the first half of my cycle I am more likely to say yes to requests for help. Oestrogen and testosterone levels rise as the body gets closer to ovulation. This boosts my mood and explains why I feel anything is possible at that time of the month. I'm also likely to make generous promises. But Gabrielle warned me that just after ovulation, the combination of dipping oestrogen and rising progesterone dampens my mood and reduces energy levels. She said, 'The second half of your cycle can turn that euphoria, that helper's high, into resentment and stress and anxiety, because now you are trying to fit it all into your already over-booked life.' She introduced me to her method for mapping the hormonal cycle in her book *28 Days: What Your Cycle Reveals about Your Moods, Health and Potential*.

186

The other side of the health story is succumbing to false needs: indulgences that offer immediate gratification. A bar of sensuous dark velvety chocolate might sound tempting but can leave you feeling guilty. Opening a bottle of wine on autopilot each night just leaves you even more tired the next day. False needs are ones that are unhealthy in the longer term. The thought, 'I need a cigarette' is about as irrational as a belief can get.

Exercise – The Foam Roller High

I keep coming back to an interview I read given by an old boy who had lived to 103 or some astronomically numbered age. When asked the secret of his longevity, his one-word answer was walking. We all know the daily recommendation is to take 10,000 steps. But did you know that walking fewer than 5,649 steps increases the risk of anxiety and depression? The average American takes 4,774. Those numbers come from *The Joy of Movement* by Kelly McGonigal. If you want to inspire yourself to do more exercise, her book is a good place to start. She emphasises finding a form of exercise that brings you joy. Movement is about social connection. You're more likely to stick at something you like and that you can do with other people. It might be exercise classes, sport or dance, whatever gets your heart pumping.

If you ever have any sort of back pain, one piece of life-changing equipment is a foam roller. Buy one now! Then simply lie along it for ten minutes. This spinal decompression trick can do wonders for the back and when you stand up (carefully) you get an exquisite rush. There are lots of other exercises you can use it for. One of my friends has to get up early to secure the roller before her kids nab it.

Psychological – Mindful or Mindless?

I've already raised a rah-rah for mindfulness and self-compassion. There are spotlights in those sections that you can try. I recommend finding an eight-week Mindfulness-Based Stress Reduction or Mindful Self-Compassion course. If you have reservations about starting to meditate you could try something I advocate on my live programmes. Simply listen to a guided meditation while you are brushing your teeth or walking the dog. One where the voice or background music appeals to you. There are plenty to choose from on various mindfulness apps. Introducing mindfulness meditation has improved my ability to intercept self-critical thoughts. It has brought other benefits, such as allowing me to reframe my nervousness and physiological arousal as excitement when I'm about to speak in public.

On the subject of managing hyper-arousal, or if you are wanting to contain your inflamed empathy circuitry, I would recommend the work of Babette Rothschild. She's a psychotherapist practitioner with a strong emphasis on psychophysiology – how the body holds trauma. She lists six stages of arousal and how changes such as heart rate, skin temperature and perspiration differ at each level. She is well known for her advice on 'putting on the brakes', a technique to develop awareness of and regulate signs of arousal in the body when exposed to a client's trauma.

Another part of meeting your psychological needs is finding support; as in the tend and befriend theory of handling stress. Reaching out to friends and family to gain (and not just give) support can deliver all those delicious oxytocic benefits. Professional support can be important too. You might want restoration, having neglected your needs to an extreme degree. You might be trying to free yourself from an unhealthy CS relationship. Or you might have resonated with what I wrote about loss of identity. You might just need someone skilled who is dedicated to listening to you. To find someone who is properly trained, professional bodies for psychologists and psychotherapists have lists of their members. One tip to save you time, money and plenty of disappointment is don't feel you have to stick to the first counsellor you sign up with. You don't want someone who asks what colour eyeshadow you use!

Finally, there's mindlessness. We all need time when we choose to do nothing, to curl up like a cat in front of the fire. Or like the cat in the lap of the woman I was coaching last night. The purring coming through my computer speakers was like a meditation. For self-preservation, bingeing on Netflix has its place. But only for as long as you aren't tricking yourself into satisfying a false need. It's only relaxing if you feel better for it, and if the pleasure balances out the guilt.

Taking time for yourself is not going to happen if you don't protect it. Nobody else is going to do that for you. I sometimes encourage my clients to book a slot in their diary as if they had a meeting with an important client. That way they prepare for it, turn up on time and are less likely to cancel at the last moment.

Home – The Matter of Matter

Having somewhere that you can call home is almost as fundamental as meeting your health needs. Before you address the higher order needs, take a look around the place where you live. Is it right for you? If you are in the right place, then the next question is, how can you make it more homely? Every helper needs somewhere snug where they can rest and replenish. Somewhere safe to retreat from the outside world. Somewhere no one asks anything of them, where they can meet their own needs. However, home can be far from relaxing for the busy helpers I've spoken to, or for those living with people they care for. I encourage them to create their own space, even if it is just a cosy corner, to be their sanctuary.

We all ignore things like creaking doors, scratched paintwork or broken lightbulbs. Each of these little annoyances don't weigh much on their own. But if you're carrying around a lot of them, the weight builds up, and every time you see the scratch or the useless lightbulb, the weight hangs heavier. Ignoring these annoyances is a classic form of self-sabotage. The value of making things right quickly is worth much more than the effort: you cast off the weight and you feel better about yourself. Invest in WD-40; buy a sample pot of paint and cover the scratches; stock up on spare lightbulbs and batteries so you have them ready in advance. Things you need in abundance. I just tried to print out the manuscript of this book and the printer cartridge was empty.

Your home can be a reflection of your essence – a part of finding your true Self. It's liberating to express yourself through the colours, textures and objects you choose to have around you. There is also the matter of matter – or clutter. Marie Kondo is the guru of the joy of folding things up really small. (It's worth watching her videos just because they are so relaxing.) Do you have a kitchen drawer crammed with old keys, junk mail and empty pens? Is there a bag of clothes you haven't taken to the charity shop? De-cluttering is a small act of self-care.

Close Relationships – Book Your Review

Research on the psychology of happiness reminds us how our overall wellbeing is related to the state of our relationships. We need to nurture them with time and effort because otherwise, like anything that's around for a long time, they start to wither. But it takes two. Both people have to invest in the partnership. If the other person isn't matching your effort, sometimes the right thing is to end it. That's sad and painful, and particularly difficult for anyone whose natural instincts are to look after those close to them. Conceding that a relationship has died takes courage, and usually requires support.

If you aren't in an intimate relationship and you want one, ask yourself are you dedicating enough time and energy to this. Would your lifestyle admit anyone else? Are you looking in the places where the right person for you is likely to be found? For now, let's assume you are in a relationship and want to strengthen it. One way to do that is to instigate what Rod and I call 'relationship reviews'. These need to be done with love and the mutual understanding that you both want to create the healthiest partnership you can. Regular reviews can bring to the surface conversations you wouldn't normally have with your partner but know you *should*. Doing this takes guts and it's the last thing either of you want to do – even when you are used to having relationship reviews and both of you are psychologists! But it has massive benefits. Maintaining broad bandwidth communication is never easy. Reviews can prevent the build-up of minor misunderstandings and irritations. They are also an opportunity to celebrate the love you share. Just doing them reminds you both how important you are to each other.

Your partner has to be the sort of person who is open to having a go at this. If they are hesitant, maybe some of the arguments above could support you in selling the idea. You could also tell them that this doesn't have to be remedial. You're not instigating the reviews because there's something wrong or because you have a particular crease to iron. In fact, the best time to introduce them is at the start when you are both loved-up and want to keep it that way.

Spotlight 9.2: *Relationship Review*

Before doing this both of you must agree that the aim is to enhance the relationship.

Ground rules can be agreed beforehand. These could include: not blaming the other person, actively listening rather than becoming defensive, and agreeing that it's okay to say whatever you want to.

1. Allocate a time with your partner. Ideally an hour.
2. Each of you in turn then talks for ten minutes.
3. During your time, you talk about the relationship and anything else you want to bring up. The other person remains completely silent.
4. You have to take your full ten minutes even if you don't know how to begin, or you want to just say, 'Everything's fine with me.'
5. After each of you has spoken you can have a more free-form discussion, clarifying and responding to what's been said and agreeing any changes you want to make.

It is important to keep a log of what is agreed. Over time the log will reveal repeated themes. It can also become a chronological archive of your journey together.

Career – A Search for Meaning

People with the No Needs Belief neglect their own careers. They dedicate all their efforts to helping others progress. Some hold themselves back deliberately, turning down management positions because they want to remain hands-on carers. But some secretly do wish to progress.

I've worked with hundreds of women, and men, afflicted by imposter syndrome. I've seen it in helpers too. They doubt how well they do their job, even when they excel at it. Their unofficial terms of employment include additional irrational beliefs, such as: 'they hired me by mistake'; 'I was the last choice candidate'; 'I'm not good enough to be here'. People with imposter syndrome dread being tapped on the shoulder and called out as a fraud. They compensate by over-striving. They take on other people's work. They turn up early and leave late. They slog away, putting in more effort than anyone else. In the end, all this leads to a promotion. When this happens they feel even more fearful. The imposter syndrome cycles on.

If this sounds familiar, try to motivate yourself out of compassion rather than fear. Maybe revisit the spotlights on the inner critic and self-compassion. Go back to the sections on claiming self-worth. Accept positive feedback at face value rather than discounting it as someone just being nice. Let go of the need for perfection and allow yourself to make mistakes. Take the pressure off; you'll still be doing a better job than everyone else.

When we find meaning in our work, we are more motivated and more productive. For helpers, meaningful work equals helping others. That frequently implies working in a caring profession. But if your work doesn't make use of your desire to help, it can be a source of frustration. One option is to change career. Another is to look for opportunities to manage or mentor people. A final way to find meaning is to reframe your work in terms of how it benefits others. Earlier we saw how pretty much any job is about helping. Here's an exercise that is used by business psychologists.

Spotlight 9.3: *Finding Meaning in Your Role*

Most role profiles list the tasks, competencies and responsibilities of the job holder.

Rewrite a description of your job from the point of view of why it exists and what value it adds.

Think about the perspective of your customers, clients, colleagues, suppliers and anyone who benefits, directly or indirectly, from what you do.

You could also think about any positive values that your organisation holds, such as sustainability, corporate social responsibility and collaboration, and how you can align your own role to those.

If you are unable to change your job or find enough meaning by reframing your role, the remaining option is to meet your needs outside work. This is covered by all the other sections in this chapter. Specifically, in relation to helping, it might mean volunteering or supporting members of your community. (But only if you are not already compulsively doing this!)

Money – You're Worth It
Many of us have an unhealthy attitude to money: too much equals guilt, not enough equals shame. What I see with helpers is they give it away ... feel guilty for having it ... don't pay attention to it ... get into debt ... never

spend it on themselves. If any of that sounds like you, I urge you to choose a different mindset. One that meets your money needs.

Now, perhaps you say it's not important; but I bet you a fiver you are the first to reach for the bill – you know money is important for others. I've worked with women who avoid opening their bank statements – yet they worry about not being in control of their finances. I mentioned before how my self-employed clients tend to under-charge for their services. If that's you, then a priority for meeting your own needs is to address this.

You might want to examine what is blocking you. A good way to start is by retelling your backstory in relation to money – what were the attitudes to money around you, and the words used for it, when you were growing up? Often it comes down to how much you value yourself. You might want to revisit the material on self-worth in Chapter 5. You might also find the section on assertiveness in the next chapter beneficial when it comes to claiming your worth with clients or employers.

Denying your need for money and all the benefits it can bring is one of the cons of the No Needs Belief. We associate money with corruption and greed, the opposites of helping. But you have as much right to an abundance as anyone else.

Spotlight 9.4: *Tracking In and Out*

One way to reduce anxiety and increase your sense of power around money is to know how much you have, where it is, when it's coming and where it's going.

Try tracking every transaction for at least one month, using a journal, a spreadsheet or one of the apps designed for this purpose.

Do you have any unexpected outgoings?

How could you reduce your spending? For example, by cancelling unnecessary subscriptions.

What do you, or could you, spend money on that brings you joy?

What, if anything, are you saving for that will enhance your longer-term wellbeing?

Waking up to your need for money management is one thing. Another is allowing yourself the freedom to enjoy what you have, and to spend it how you want.

Fun – Welcome to the Glow Festival

Going back to my favourite guru on helping, Friedrich Nietzsche tells us, 'Truly, I did this and that for the afflicted; but it always seemed to me I did better things when I learned to enjoy myself better.' For many helpers, fun is so far down their list of priorities it has disappeared completely from view. All their effort goes into making sure other people are having fun – organising a birthday treat for their best friend, entertaining the kids in the garden. Their helper's guilt kicks in if they spend time on themselves.

The trick is to find healthful ways to have a good time. That's a challenge for those who have busy lives or who work in pressured or distressing environments. It can be tempting to let off steam by resorting to the false needs I mentioned in the section on health.

If much of your life is spent looking after people with 'serious' problems, it's hard to switch off the responsible, dutiful, earnest, solemn, preoccupied adult mode. You forget how to switch on the playful, relaxed, silly, happy, carefree, childlike mode. You may even judge these as irresponsible or undesirable states. But don't frown on fun. We all have an innate capacity for laughter and joy. And they are good for you. In her book *Laughology*, the comedian Stephanie Davies lists all the health benefits of laughter, including boosting your immune system, relaxing the muscles and improving sleep. I had a chortle with her on a video call recently when she told me about some of the techniques she uses. She has a 'joke jar' in her kitchen that she fills with funny snippets 'that I can open when I want to feel more childlike or for inspiration. We all have sayings or silly jokes or songs from our childhood that transport us straight back to that childlike place.'

If you want to reconnect with your childlike self, the first thing to do is give yourself permission. It can also be liberating to spend time with actual children (if you're not already a frazzled parent or working in paediatrics!). Hanging out with them gives you an excuse to delight in the little things. One evening, on a recent camping trip, my 8-year-old niece and I put on the Glow Festival, complete with tiaras, bangles and waistbands, all made from glow sticks.

Another way to find the fun part deep within you is to go back to what you chose to do as a child. Did you love to collect things or kick a ball about? Or maybe sing, dance or paint? There are adult classes for all sorts of things. When people craft the persona of their inner critic, they say they love that exercise because it brings out their inner child. If you feel brave enough, you could try improvisation drama. You learn how to play again and learn not to care whether what you are doing is any good. It only matters that it's fun, and it's actually funniest when you mess up. Fun means different things to different people. If all your attention has been on others you may not have a clear idea of what makes you happy. Here's an exercise to reconnect with this.

Spotlight 9.5: *Having a Laugh*

Give yourself a couple of minutes to answer the following questions. Try not to overthink it. Just write down what first comes to mind.

What makes you laugh?
Who makes you laugh?
If you could do anything this weekend, what would you do?
What's the most fun you've ever had?
If you could go anywhere in the world, where would you go?
If you found a treasure chest with your name on it, what would it contain?

Community – Gemeinschaftsgefühl

As a helper, even a healthy one, you inevitably give a lot to the people in your life. If you are to meet your own needs too, it's vital to know at least a few people that contribute as much to you: those who buoy you up. They are your friends. With them, the relationship isn't primarily about you helping them. Your friends help you in equal measure. That's the rule for the healthy helper – the principle of reciprocity is key here. Anyone who is your friend because you are helping them, is not your friend.

To be stomach-tighteningly honest with yourself about the people in your life, categorise them – helpees vs. friends. I realise that you might feel guilty about depersonalising them like this. It's certainly not something I would suggest for everyone, only those who are compulsive helpers. It's just a private thought experiment for you to try. To do this in a more structured way, you could work through the following spotlight.

Spotlight 9.6: *Friendometer*

Think about one person in your life at a time and answer the following questions	I do	About equal	They do
1. Who helps the other the most?			
2. Who initiates contact the most?			
3. Who asks the most questions?			
4. Who remembers details about the other's life?			
5. Who encourages the other the most?			
6. Who shows that they are always there for the other?			

If you answered 'I do' to Question 1 above, I hope you took a deep breath and then gently lowered them into the helpee bucket and started again with another potential friend. If you continue a relationship with someone you thought was a friend but now realise is a helpee, that's your choice. At least it's a conscious one now. But you can't do that with everyone. Without at least a few friends who give as much to the relationship as you do, you will end up back in exhaustion and resentment.

Some of us have a wide network of contacts or Facebook 'friends'. But casual contacts aren't in a position to offer deep support. Those aren't friends in the way we've discussed here. The list of friends I'm talking about is always going to be a short one. Anyone battling the No Needs Belief has to learn to nurture and enjoy those true friendships.

I certainly don't want to play down the value of a broader sense of community. That's a need we have too. Remember Alfred Adler's idea of social interest, *Gemeinschaftsgefühl*. It's something that is often missing in modern life, especially the anonymity of urban life. Since I relocated to a rural area, the thing that has most delighted me is discovering a sense of community. I expected the air to be cleaner and I knew we would be surrounded by hills, but I could never have known how friendly my neighbours would be. I've already mentioned the street barbecues. If your needs for community aren't being met, I would urge you to seek out your own tribe or group of like-minded people where you belong.

Aspirational – What Comes Next?

It's only by growing that we stay alive. It's only by growing that we flourish. That's true for any living organism: plants, animals, people. For human beings that means learning. We've all watched a baby circumnavigate the room, cruising from the coffee table to the sofa, eyes wide and alert to every new stimulation. We've seen their joy at pointing at and naming objects. Later, when passing an exam, or queuing left of stage to be handed a degree certificate. Some of the proudest moments. Or running a thumb over the embossed name on a membership card from a respected professional body. Times when we feel most alive. Later still, studying a language or taking up a musical instrument keeps the neurons fired up and can even ward off dementia. Learning is one of our defining features and has taken us to incredible heights of art and science.

> Ever tried. Ever failed. No matter. Try again. Fail again. Fail better.
>
> Samuel Beckett, *Worstward Ho*

But if you've been suffering from Super-Helper Syndrome, your aspirational needs will be gathering dust in the loft. Helpers often only develop skills that allow them to be better at helping others. In Chapter 6, I mentioned how an addiction to attaining helping-related qualifications can be a tell-tale sign of the Help Everyone Belief. Here, I'd like to invite you to think more broadly about what you want to learn for your own sake.

Here's a random list to get you started: archery, ballroom dancing, calligraphy, divining, embroidery, flame-throwing, growing vegetables, hang-gliding, improvisation, juggling, karate, life-drawing, macramé, Norwegian, origami, phillumeny, quoits, rowing, singing, tennis, ukulele, videography, windsurfing, xeriscaping, yarn bombing, zorbing.

Spotlight 9.7: *From Potholing to Playwriting*

What would you like to learn?

How can you go about learning this? Are there opportunities to skill-swap, borrow or hire equipment, join a taster session, ask for a birthday gift?

You could set an overall goal with short-term targets to motivate yourself. And don't forget to have fun!

If you are keen to kick-start your learning, it's easy to be too ambitious. You can end up with a long list. You become the *Yes Man* that Jim Carrey played, agreeing to every suggestion. He simultaneously took up learning guitar, Korean language classes and flying lessons, amid a host of other activities. It's a good idea to concentrate on just one or two things at first that you will actually stick to. You can always come back to the others later.

Taking a broader view of aspirational needs means thinking about your hopes for the future. It's invigorating to have big ideas, exciting plans, dreams. You don't have to share them with anyone. You can always rewrite them tomorrow.

Spotlight 9.8: *Dare to Dream*

What do you want your life to look like in five to ten years? Consider all the needs listed above, and think about the person you want to become.

> Who do you want to be?
> What do you want to do?
> Where do you want to be?
> Who do you want to be with?
> How do you want to feel?

That final question, which asks you to set an emotional goal, how you want to feel, is perhaps the most important. It's the one thing all the others should be feeding in to. Check that your answers to the first four questions will lead you in the direction of your emotional goal.

Soul – When Faerie Invades the World

Balanced at the tip of the tree of needs there's just one more. The need for meaning in life; personal fulfilment, spiritual satisfaction – whatever soul means to you. In Chapter 5 we looked at the quest to find your true Self. That was a core part of Robert Hartman's philosophy on knowing yourself to be good. Your soul needs relate directly to the expression of your true Self. They are as individual as you are. They might mean alignment to a charitable or political cause. Or belonging to a faith or community group. They might be found in close connection to family or friends. Or immersing yourself in the magnificence of the mountains, trees, lakes or the sea. Or pausing in the quiet of prayer, ritual or meditation. Or moving to the rhythm of dance or yoga. Or expressing the agony and the joy of humanity through poetry, art or music. Or taking on a grand endeavour – building your Sagrada Familia.

One way into this is to start from your values. If you are a helper then some of those are predictably about connection, compassion, community and so on. But you are more than that. Take a moment to uncover your hidden values.

Spotlight 9.9: *Your Hidden Values*

You might have seen lists like this before, but here I've already given you the values that are the most obvious for helpers (in bold). Read through the list and highlight the ones that resonate with you – cross out any that definitely do not. Go through this process until you have at least five in addition to the helper ones.

Acceptance	Effort	Intellect
Achievement	Enthusiasm	Intimacy
Adventure	Environment	Inventiveness
Aesthetics	**Equality**	Joy
Ambition	Expertise	Justice
Analysis	Exploration	**Kindness**
Art	**Fairness**	Knowledge
Assertiveness	Faith	Leadership
Authenticity	Family	Learning
Belonging	Fitness	**Love**
Celebration	Freedom	Loyalty
Charity	**Friendship**	Music
Commitment	Frugality	Nature
Community	Fun	**Nurturing**
Compassion	**Generosity**	Openness
Competence	Growth	Optimism
Competition	Harmony	Patience
Connection	Health	Peace
Conscientiousness	**Helping**	Perfection
Courage	History	Philosophy
Creativity	Honesty	Pleasure
Culture	Humility	Power
Curiosity	Humour	Protection
Democracy	Inclusiveness	Punctuality
Discipline	Independence	Relaxation
Diversity	Individuality	Routine
Efficiency	Integrity	Science

Security	Strength	Truth
Simplicity	Success	Vitality
Spirituality	Tolerance	Wealth
Spontaneity	Tradition	Wildlife
Status	Trust	Wisdom

Now reflect on the following questions:

To what extent can you express these values in your life?
If are they missing, where could you find them?

Another way to open up to your soul is through stories:

One story I will try to reproduce. But, alas! it is like trying to reconstruct a forest out of broken branches and withered leaves. In the fairy book, everything was just as it should be, though whether in words or something else, I cannot tell. It glowed and flashed the thoughts upon the soul, with such a power that the medium disappeared from the consciousness, and it was occupied only with the things themselves. My representation of it must resemble a translation from a rich and powerful language, capable of embodying the thoughts of a splendidly developed people, into the meagre and half-articulate speech of a savage tribe. Of course, while I read it, I was Cosmo, and his history was mine. Yet, all the time, I seemed to have a kind of double consciousness, and the story a double meaning. Sometimes it seemed only to represent a simple story of ordinary life, perhaps almost of universal life; wherein two souls, loving each other and longing to come nearer, do, after all, but behold each other as in a glass darkly. As through the hard rock go the branching silver veins; as into the solid land run the creeks and gulfs from the unresting sea; as the lights and influences of the upper worlds sink silently through the earth's atmosphere; so doth Faerie invade the world of men, and sometimes startle the common eye with an association as of cause and effect, when between the two no connecting links can be traced.

George MacDonald, *Phantastes*

201

Siddhartha bent down, lifted a stone from the ground and held it in his hand. 'This,' he said, handling it, 'is a stone, and within a certain length of time it will perhaps be soil and from the soil it will become plant, animal or man. Previously I should have said: This stone is just a stone; it has no value, it belongs to the world of Maya, but perhaps because within the cycle of change it can also become man and spirit, it is also of importance. That is what I should have thought. But now I think: This stone is stone; it is also animal, God and Buddha. I do not respect and love it because it was one thing and will become something else, but because it has already long been everything and always is everything. I love it just because it is a stone, because today and now it appears to me a stone. I see value and meaning in each one of its fine markings and cavities, in the yellow, in the grey, in the hardness and the sound of it when I knock it, in the dryness or dampness of its surface. There are stones that feel like oil or soap, that look like leaves or sand, and each one is different and worships Om in its own way; each one is Brahman. At the same time it is very much stone, oily or soapy, and that is just what pleases me and seems wonderful and worthy of worship.'

Hermann Hesse, *Siddhartha*

Chapter 10

The Hardy Helper

Now we have created the conditions for healthy helping, the next chapter of this survival guide has to be about self-preservation. How to protect healthy helpers. I'll look at what's on offer from psychological research in the fields of stress and hardiness. We'll revisit some of the situations where self-preservation is most challenging – when dealing with trauma. Finally, we come to the most protective piece of equipment available to helpers – effective boundaries.

Is Stress Bad?

The dominant story in science and in the press has been that stress leads to cardiovascular disease and a host of other health conditions. That's the story we have all bought into. Whenever we are overwhelmed by life we blame it on stress. (We don't blame our compulsive helping.) We take holidays to reduce stress. We take time off work with stress. It's everywhere and many of us worry about its effects.

For helpers it comes with a side order of guilt. They feel guilty when they struggle to handle the pressure. They feel guilty if they take time off, leaving overburdened colleagues to carry on. It's the G word yet again. The people

I interviewed even reproached themselves for having helper's guilt. One said, 'I know it's a first world problem; I should be able to cope.' They told me taking time off for stress is pointless. They can't switch off at home. They might as well stay at work.

The common wisdom has long been that we should try to avoid stress. As Kelly McGonigal puts it in her book, *The Upside of Stress*:

> When I shared scary statistics about stress with caregivers, sometimes there were tears. No matter the audience, nobody ever came up afterwards to say, 'Thank you so much for telling me how toxic my stressful life is. I know I can get rid of the stress, but I'd just never thought to do it before!'

A whole industry has jumped on the back of the view that stress is bad: stress-management programmes that have little impact. Despite this, among my business psychology colleagues, I hardly know anyone who hasn't run this sort of thing, albeit with the best of intentions. The programmes typically start off with a gruelling first hour, trudging through all sorts of alarming and depressing stats about how stress is bad for you. It's all valid research, but how does it help to hear it? We end up stressed about stress. There's also the risk that this type of training can be used as a bandage, taping over the wound when management aren't prepared to provide the resources and supportive culture people need. Instead, they summon a psychologist to put everyone through a one-day course. But much of the stress we experience can't be ameliorated by stress-management techniques alone. Many of us cannot avoid working in high-pressure or distressing environments. Even if the techniques are sound, there's no time to apply them, and they don't alter the work environment. Besides, some stress comes from events we don't want to avoid. Some of the best things we do in life are stressful, like moving house, getting married, having a child, writing a book. Without stress, life would be dull. What most of us haven't heard is that there's another side to stress. That it can be good for you. That you can be hardy.

The Power of Hardiness

The idea of 'hardiness' came from psychologists who studied how people react to stressful situations. The term was first taken up by Suzanne Kobasa, a graduate student at the University of Chicago in the 1970s. She conducted what is now a legendary piece of research at the Illinois Bell Telephone Company. The organisation was going through turmoil as a result of deregulation of the industry. In one year, the company reduced its staff by almost half, terminating about 12,000 employees. Kobasa and her supervisor Salvatore Maddi studied the individuals affected by this upheaval. They found that two-thirds of them 'fell apart', showing the signs of stress that you might expect: depression, drug dependency, divorces, heart attacks, strokes, cancers, suicide. However, the remaining third actually thrived, whether they were made redundant or not. They told the researchers that they experienced more fulfilment than they had before. This led Maddi to propose that how people interpreted the stressful events in their lives mattered more than the severity of the adverse experiences they faced:

> ... hardiness gives you the courage to face stresses, turn them to your advantage, and grow in the process.
>
> Salvatore Maddi, *Hardiness*

The Bell Telephone study inspired a wealth of research showing the advantages of hardiness. Much of this has tracked people over time to see how their attitudes to stress affect their health. Norwegian police trainees, for example, were put in a simulation where they had to respond to a gunman. Those who were high in hardiness reacted with initially increased signs of stress but then calmed down sooner than those low in hardiness. Another study in Norway tracked hundreds of nurses over a two-year period. Those who were lower in hardiness tended to experience more fatigue, anxiety and depression. In Morocco, hardiness profiles were collected from nurses and doctors at the Ibn Sina Hospital. Those who were hardier had lower incidences of stress-related illnesses such as hypertension.

Hardy people still experience the stress but handle it better. In the literature on hardiness they are defined by three characteristics. They have a strong sense of purpose in life. They respond to challenges as opportunities to grow. They believe they have control over their own destinies; that they can have an impact on the world. In their recent book *Hardiness*, Steven Stein and Paul Bartone write, 'The authentic (hardy) person regularly chooses the path of engagement and active involvement in the world, instead of the relative safety of passive withdrawal and inaction.'

In traumatising work environments hardy people are more likely to resort to gallows humour. This creates a bond among colleagues going through horrific experiences together and it displays a stoic, I-can-handle-this mindset. Firefighters in Los Angeles who were higher in hardiness tended to make jokes about matters of life and death. The same has been found with wounded soldiers returning from Iraq and Afghanistan. It's a staple of war films. In my interviews, several of the intensive care nurses mentioned this. After calling her ward a war zone, one of them said, 'Black humour helps a lot – we say some horrible things [giggles guiltily] but it just helps you through ... otherwise you'd go home and cut your throat [laughs].' She admitted this to me with a note of shame in her voice. But gallows humour can be an effective psychological coping mechanism. If you use it, you don't need to be ashamed of it.

Can You Become Hardier?

There is plenty of data showing that hardiness is a great quality to have. But is it something you are born with, or can it be learned? And if it can be learned, how do you get your hands on some?

When I first introduced the idea of irrational beliefs, I also mentioned the work of Alia Crum. You recall – mindsets, housemaids and milkshakes? She and her colleagues have also carried out research on mindset in relation to stress. They too have been challenging the prevailing view that it's bad for you, de facto. They stress the benefits of stress. It has been linked with enhanced cognitive performance, personal initiative and emotional stability. It can promote physiological thriving, enhanced immunity and faster healing.

How you are affected by stress is determined to a large extent by how you think about it – mindset. In one wacky experiment, scientists from the University of Barcelona studied Catalans bungee jumping off a bridge. They did this because previous research had shown that stressful situations impair concentration and memory. But those were all situations where the stress was perceived as negative. Bungee jumping gave them the chance to observe people taking part in a stressful activity, with racing hearts and all the other signs of stress, but where they were having fun. The researchers actually found that performance on a memory task, recalling a list of digits, was improved when people were hyped up after the jump.

Crum and her colleagues have looked at stress mindset in a variety of settings including those who work in one of the most challenging environments: Navy SEALs. They have been in the news for exploits such as rescuing a cargo ship from Somali pirates, or, most famously, the killing of Osama bin Laden. SEALs face notoriously tough training that includes 'Hell Week'. During that time, candidates complete tasks and drills almost non-stop and are allowed only forty-five minutes of sleep per night. Fewer than 20 per cent of those who start the training complete it successfully. Alia Crum and her colleagues showed that SEAL candidates with a mindset that they called 'stress is enhancing' were more likely to make it.

Scientists have also shown that this mindset can be cultivated. Mindset interventions have altered university students' perception of stress, leading to improved exam performance. Interventions have also enabled students to cope better with social isolation during the first year of college. In the workplace, Crum studied a group of employees at UBS during the 2008 economic crash. Much like the Illinois Bell Telephone Company, but more than thirty years later, UBS was going through a massive drop in its financial performance and was shedding large numbers of staff. Employees were invited to participate in stress-management training and were divided into three groups. One group was given a 'stress-is-debilitating' intervention, comprising a series of three-minute videos and an online training session telling them things like stress is linked to six leading causes of death. One group was given a 'stress-is-enhancing' intervention. This included messages such as stress helps you perform better, learn to utilise it, learn to enjoy it. The third group was given no training at all. Those who were trained to believe that stress is enhancing had reduced muscle tension and insomnia, fewer headaches and less hypertension. Their work performance also improved in comparison with the other two groups.

As I mentioned in relation to the Healthy Helper Mindset, these sorts of interventions tend to stick. The benefits can even be cumulative. The students with a stress-is-enhancing mindset actually did better in their second-year exams without any further interventions. That is encouraging: once you see the benefits that result from a new mindset, that in itself can reinforce the new set of beliefs. There's no need for a top-up.

Mindset interventions don't deny the harmful effects of stress. Where hormones and other physiological indicators have been measured, these show that the interventions do not necessarily reduce the level of stress. They limit the damage. The best interventions don't simply foist a propaganda message on you: 'Stress is good for you.' They set out the evidence for both sides of the argument and allow you to choose. Given that believing that stress is bad for you only makes things worse, wouldn't you choose a mindset that stress can be useful?

Spotlight 10.1: *Stress Makes You Stronger*

To adopt a stress-is-enhancing mindset, remind yourself that you can choose how to respond to stressful situations. Use the following prompts to affirm this new way of thinking:

'I've dealt with stress in the past and it's made me stronger.'
'Stressful situations prepare me for peak performance.'
'When my heart races, my mouth goes dry and I have butterflies in my tummy, those are all signs I'm gearing up to perform my best.'
'Challenges are exciting and bring out the best in me.'
'I can handle anything that comes my way.'

These statements are based on scientific evidence and can all be true for you. It's a matter of believing them, rather than trying to drum them into your brain by mindless repetition.

During exercise, muscles need to be torn in order to rebuild stronger. Vaccines stress your body so that it fights back and gains immunity. You can use other stressors in the same way.

The knowledge that you have overcome difficult times in the past can support you when you face future challenges.

Spotlight 10.2: *Find Strength from Stress*

Bring to mind a stressful situation that you have survived. Focus on what gave you the strength to come through. What attitudes helped? Which aspects of your personality supported you? What did you do that helped you cope?

Notice any ways that you became more resilient as a result of the situation. Harness this to remind yourself that whatever you face today … you can make it … this too will pass … you will come out stronger.

But What About Trauma?

If you work in the face of trauma, all this talk about befriending stress might still sound unrealistic. Nobody should deny the difficulties, but there is hope. There are plenty of well-documented examples to show that human beings can thrive even in the darkest moments: everything from bereavement to house fires to being held hostage, and a range of severe illnesses. Beth Hudnall Stamm worked as a consultant on a psychotherapeutic programme supporting survivors of violence in South Africa. Observing the therapists delivering that programme, she found that most of them pressed on, 'often with joy', rather than succumbing to compassion fatigue. This led her to develop the concept of 'compassion satisfaction', an expansion of the theory that was encouraged and supported by Charles Figley. She describes this as 'happiness with what one can do to make the world in which one lives a reflection of what one thinks it should be'. It's an apt reminder of the eudaimonistic judgement element of compassion. Stamm also proposed that hardiness plays an important role for professional carers who work with traumatised patients. There was more risk of compassion fatigue when they felt they couldn't influence the outcome and when they felt less equipped to cope with the patient's trauma. Some people come through stronger and with a renewed purpose in life. That phenomenon has also been called 'post-traumatic growth'. No matter how distressing your situation, believing that the stress is hurting you cannot help.

In the chapter on the unhealthy helper, I mentioned that compassion fatigue drags people away from effective caring in one of two directions. Some become toughened and lose their empathy. Others take on the burden of suffering and lose themselves. The answer lies in finding a middle way, a balance where the helper is able to act with compassion and also protect themselves. If you are concerned about whether you or someone you know is suffering with compassion fatigue you could look at *Trauma Stewardship* by social worker Laura van Dernoot Lipsky. She provides vivid descriptions of sixteen signs to test whether you are experiencing compassion fatigue. She draws on her own story of being overwhelmed by trauma in a hospital emergency room and her subsequent spiritual journey. Her emphasis is on self-awareness and staying present.

Another invaluable resource is the huge range of worksheets, self-assessments, checklists and exercises provided by William Steele. He started working in child suicide and has gone on to be one of the world leaders in the area of reducing compassion fatigue. He has trained thousands of people and his methods have been applied in major disasters such as the Oklahoma bombing, 9/11 and Hurricane Katrina.

Whether it is everyday helpers coping with Super-Helper Syndrome or professional carers facing compassion fatigue, the methods to protect helpers are broadly similar to the ones I've covered in this book: mindfulness, finding meaning, self-compassion, meeting your own needs, humour, hardiness and ...

Boundaries, Dahling!

Now we come to possibly the most powerful piece of equipment to protect the healthy helper. All of the irrational beliefs that underpin the Super-Helper

Syndrome prevent someone from establishing boundaries. In particular, they make it impossible to say no to requests for help. A lack of boundaries leads to all the adverse impacts: exhaustion, resentment, exploitation and self-criticism. By contrast, the alternative beliefs were designed to lay the foundations on which you can build effective boundaries:

'My self-worth is not dependent on helping others.'
'I know and respect the limits of my capacity to help.'
'I know and respect the limits of my responsibility to help.'
'I deserve to have my own needs met.'

These alternative beliefs create the possibility for you to say no. They encourage you to *respect* boundaries with regard to when and how much you help, not going beyond your *capacity* or your *responsibility* to do so, and not helping when it will leave you unable to meet your own *needs*. So, let's set some boundaries.

Identifying Boundaries – Who, How, When?

Unless you sit down and think through them deliberately, there's close to zero chance you will set any. Start by referring back to Spotlight 3.1 or 6.1 or make a list of all the people that you're helping now.

Think about *who* you are going to help. You need to be honest with yourself about all the people you are currently helping. Are there some who are just draining you? Are there some who are exploiting you? Are there some who rely on you unnecessarily? You may even need to jettison a few false friends who are really just helpees. They might be the ones you identified in the Friendometer (Spotlight 9.6). There might be other people in your life who hinder you from meeting your own needs. You might need to let go of them too. At one point, in the name of self-preservation, I made a conscious decision to sever connection with my father. That was painful but setting boundaries isn't easy. (He didn't seem to mind!)

Think about *how* you are going to help. You might decide that the helping you do as part of your paid job is enough. Perhaps you will only offer a particular person supportive help but not resources help, or vice versa.

Think about *when* you are going to help. You might limit the time you give to certain people. You might decide to listen to your mother's problems when you see her for Sunday lunches, but not spend time on the phone to her when you are at work. You might allocate some protected time for yourself each week.

Spotlight 10.3: *Choose Your Helping Boundaries*

Who do you choose to help?
How do you choose to help?
When do you choose to help?

As well as helping boundaries, if you're going to have any chance of meeting your own needs, you've got to establish lifestyle boundaries. Use Spotlight 10.4 to go through the list of categories of needs from the last chapter and identify any areas you want to protect. Sometimes it's easier to pinpoint the things you don't want. Boundaries keep things out as well as keeping things in. You might not have anything to write in many of the rows, but it's a good idea to set a few conscious boundaries if you can. Here are some examples to prompt you ...

Spotlight 10.4 *Choose Your Lifestyle Boundaries*

	Examples of Conscious Boundaries
Health Diet, health check-ups, drinking, smoking, self-medicating	I'll only drink alcohol at the weekend.
Exercise Walking, gym, exercise classes, sport, dance	I'll protect Tuesday nights for my yoga class.
Psychological Rest, relaxation, meditation, talking to someone, coaching, counselling	When I take annual leave I'll make sure that it is truly restful.

Home Providing and maintaining a home that feels safe, comfortable, uncluttered	I'll stop picking up the wet towels on the bathroom floor that are driving me crazy.
Close Relationships Maintaining healthy relationships with people who love and respect you: partner, family	I will commit to turning up for our relationship reviews rather than cancelling them.
Career Working hours, levels of stress, work satisfaction, career development	I won't work more than **x** number of hours each week.
Money Income, debt, outgoings	I'll stop lending money to **X**.
Fun Hobbies, holidays, adventures	I will always take **x** weeks of annual leave each year.
Community Belonging, safety, spending time with people who support you rather than drain you	I'll limit my time with **X**.
Aspirational Personal growth, working towards being the best version of yourself	I'll implement a five-year life plan.
Soul Finding meaning in life, spiritual satisfaction, faith, creativity	I'll protect time for meditation each week.

Again, it's a good idea not to take on too much. For now, choose three life-style boundaries you can immediately act upon.

Protecting Boundaries – The Zorb of Zen

If you have a suffering friend, be a resting-place for his suffering,
but a resting place like a hard bed, a camp-bed; thus you will serve him best.
Nietzsche, *Thus Spoke Zarathustra*

And thus, you will protect your boundaries! One way to protect conscious boundaries is to tell people about them in advance. But often you haven't deliberately thought about them or written them down in the way that we've tried to do here. People have unconscious boundaries too. Those are the sort that only trip and set off alarms when they are breached. You experience a sense of unease, exposure, wrongness. You don't like someone else's behaviour towards you. You feel compromised. And when that happens, whether the boundaries are conscious or unconscious, it's essential to act. That takes assertiveness.

As we know, helpers seldom attend to their own needs, let alone stand up for themselves. So being assertive is not even on the menu. Some of them worry that they might become aggressive. It's easy to get confused about the difference between assertiveness and aggressiveness so here's a simple two-by-two grid that illustrates this.

Their Rights Protected	Submissive	Assertive
Their Rights Not Protected	Avoidant	Aggressive
	My Rights Not Protected	My Rights Protected

Assertiveness is standing up for your own rights without trampolining on the rights of the other person. Someone who has habitually acted in a submissive or avoidant manner is extremely unlikely to turn into an aggressive person. People with Super-Helper Syndrome have habitually protected other people's rights while ignoring their own (the submissive quadrant in the grid). The idea that they might suddenly become aggressive – protecting their own rights and ignoring other people's – suggests an incredible volte-face. It's another irrational fear. We've been struck by the Full Moon Phobia again. The very fact that you might be worried about becoming aggressive shows that it could never happen. In fact, those who are recovering from Super-Helper Syndrome are so nice and accommodating they can typically get away with being as blunt as they dare (which isn't very). The people around you might be surprised that you are being assertive but they are unlikely to think that you're being rude or aggressive. If you do hear yourself occasionally snap at others, it doesn't mean you're an aggressive person. It could be a sign of a build-up of helper's resentment. In any case, rather than labelling or criticising yourself for it, forgive yourself and keep working on developing assertiveness.

Charlie is the mother of twin girls at primary school. She chooses to be self-employed as a virtual assistant so she can work at home and be there for her family. Recently, one of the other women, with a daughter in the same class, lost her mother-in-law. She asked Charlie to pick up her daughter from school and take care of her in the afternoons. Charlie (trying to set some boundaries) agreed to do this for a short time until the woman found a new arrangement. She also agreed to look after the girl for a maximum of two hours each day (trying to set more boundaries). After a week or so, the woman 'started to take the mickey by popping to the shops on the way home and turning up late without even checking if I had plans'. Charlie was frustrated because she ended up not having any post-school downtime with her own girls. She was constantly on the go until clearing up after dinner. As time went by, there was no sign of the woman making new childcare arrangements. Charlie mentioned this to a mutual friend who 'gossiped it back to the other lady and she has never spoken to me since'. This was 'a pretty crap ending to a situation where I was only trying to help'.

Her experience is characteristic of compulsive helping as well as an example of not protecting boundaries. In fact, it neatly shows up all four of the main adverse impacts of the Super-Helper Syndrome. Charlie told me she was exhausted. She expressed resentment to the mutual friend, because her helping tendencies were exploited. And in our interview Charlie was self-critical, blaming herself. Looking at the two-by-two grid above, her behaviour was avoidant. She didn't talk to the woman who was overstepping her boundaries, but she did talk to the mutual friend. Let's look at all four options that were available to her.

Avoidant: Allow the situation to continue, say nothing or only speak to someone else.

Submissive: Ask the woman if she's made new childcare arrangements and when she says she hasn't, agree to keep looking after her daughter.

Aggressive: Tell her, I'm not looking after your bloody daughter any more. She's still at school now; go and pick her up yourself.

Assertive: Tell her a fixed date by which you will stop looking after her daughter. Check that she understands this. Remind her just before the deadline. Then stop looking after her daughter. (Do not get involved in finding alternative childcare solutions for her.)

Learning to be assertive in protecting your boundaries takes time and practice. And courage. You have to start getting used to meeting your own needs first. You need to build up your confidence and the belief that you have rights. Your behaviour has to match what you feel inside, otherwise you will crumble at the first push back from others when you try to assert yourself. They will be able to tell that you don't really have faith in yourself. For this reason, you might want to practise in a safe environment with close family and friends first rather than tackling your mortal enemy on day one.

Here's a thought experiment: An old friend of yours has recently split up with her partner. She phones to ask if she can come and stay at your house for a short while.

How do you say no?

If you're a compulsive helper that probably wasn't the first option that came to mind. Your knee-jerk reaction was to say yes and rush off to put fresh linen on the spare bed. But coming back to asserting your boundaries, how do you say no? Again, if you're a compulsive helper you start list-ing excuses in your head that you could offer: 'I'd love to help but it's not convenient right now'; 'Bad timing, we're just having the spare bedroom redecorated'; 'Josh has invited his elderly mother to stay, and she's arriv-ing tomorrow'. Of course, if you were going to refuse, you would have your reasons for doing so, but you don't always have to give your reasons. What I find fascinating is that knowing nothing about the background – the state of your relationship with her, why she's split up with her husband, whether or not it is practical for you to offer her a bed – you feel obligated to help. Knowing nothing about the situation, you still feel uncomfortable saying no. What if I told you that she'd previously had an affair with Josh? Does that make it easier to say no? Someone with Super-Helper Syndrome would probably still be tempted to help.

It takes assertiveness to say no. It is difficult, but it is within your rights. There are also situations where the power balance of the relationship makes it nigh on impossible to simply say no – when your boss asks for something, for example.

Here are some slightly less drastic tactics:

Offer alternatives – 'Ask Marie, she's got three spare bedrooms.'
Buy time – 'I'll let you know once I've spoken to Josh.'
Don't apologise – 'It's not convenient for us at the moment.'

Spotlight 10.5: *Boundaries Role Model*

Role modelling is a powerful way to adopt new behaviours. It's how we pick up much of what we learn as children. Find someone you respect, who is good at establishing and protecting their boundaries. Someone who does it in a skilled, assertive way. Observe how and when they do this and what the results are. Make notes on the language they use, how they use non-verbal communication and any other techniques.

If you feel comfortable and you trust them, you could also ask them how they learned to protect their boundaries.

Spotlight 10.6: *Just Say No*

This is a simple and quick exercise.
Say no the next five times you are asked for help.
You are not allowed to give any reasons. Don't say, 'I can't do that.'
Simply say, 'No. I won't do that.'

Okay, not really! The final spotlight in this book is not for real. It's just an experiment. What's interesting is how it made you feel. Did the very idea of saying no unnerve you? If so, was it the same sense of unease you feel when your boundaries are being breached? Ironically, that would be the boundary 'I shouldn't say no'. And I breached it just by getting you to read Spotlight 10.6. If one of your boundaries is that you should never say no, it shows how you can have boundaries that are unconscious and unhealthy for you. The spotlight didn't ask you to be aggressive or rude. You are within your rights to say no. Remember to be honest with yourself and admit when your boundaries have been breached. Have the courage to stand up for yourself. Protecting boundaries takes vigilance and integrity.

Boundaries are the Zorb of Zen to keep you safe from the Super-Helper Syndrome. If you don't know, zorbing is where you roll down a hill inside a transparent plastic bubble. I've tried it, and it's great fun. Here's another thought experiment that I use with my clients. Imagine yourself safe and comfortable inside your zorb. You can still interact with the world as normal, but it slows your reactions down. It gives you the opportunity to observe others from within your zorb when they are throwing their emotions at you like wet paper tissues. It prevents you from immediately taking on other people's drama or instinctively giving in to your urge to help. You can use the Zorb of Zen to shield you from toxic situations that others want to draw you into. It gives you the time to choose how to respond. You don't have to absorb their emotions. You watch them slide down the outside of your zorb like wet paper tissues.

Chapter 11

The Compassionate Life

The sun was breaking through segments of cloud to paint the shoulders of Rinjani a soft pink. It was a sight to see but that wasn't why I was up so early. We never climbed that mountain. The weather wasn't right. It had rained every day and all that night; water dancing off the matted roof of our lumbung hut, dripping from the eaves onto the muddy, froggy ground and the rough decking where I was sitting. I'd stared at the upside-down geckos on the bamboo rafters much of the night, but that wasn't the reason I was up so early.

I was working. At least in theory. Or berating myself for not working. The journal I'd lugged around Bali, Lombok and the Gilis was heavy in my lap but not heavy with words. I'd managed to write a few descriptions of our treks: waterfalls and rainforest. I'd written a note not to eat raw jackfruit because the guide said it would make my tummy go boom, boom, boom. I'd painted in words the woman who invited us into a hut for winnowing grain, who gave us hot purple potatoes she roasted in a pot on an open fire.

I was supposed to be writing a book about women who were nulliparous by choice, those who, like me, didn't want to have children. With a mother and father like mine, I'd decided it best to draw a line. In any event, I'd inherited a son from the man who was still asleep in the hut behind me. A son who would never be my son, but who I would always love. I wanted to help women who felt under pressure to have children. I'd interviewed brilliant, determined, self-critical women, but couldn't seem to get started on the book. I never climbed that mountain.

As usual my career was at a crossroads. I'd recently started as an independent business psychologist and later that day I would fly back to England so I could help a healthcare company build a better management team. But was it enough? I wanted to do more to help more people. Perhaps I should tell myself to count my blessings! Perhaps it was just the strange existential awareness that came from sitting in a foreign dawn, in just pyjama shorts and T-shirt, looking out over the steaming rice paddies, under the massive, brooding eye of Rinjani. The volcano stared down, disapproving of me. Other women were already out in the fields. One trudged the clay path between the paddies, a yoke and two bales saddled on her back. Was I the only one not working this morning?

My mother taught me to be a helper. Not to help anyone else, mind. She conditioned me to look after number one: that meant her. It's no surprise that I joined the National Health Service. When I got back from building the proboscis monkey research centre at Camp Leakey in Borneo I started my training as a psychologist. I found the first of my clinical placements by volunteering in a psychiatric unit alongside doing bar work and housekeeping, so I had money to pay rent to my mother. I'd come back to live with her for a while as a pit stop until I could sort out somewhere else, so I was her live-in carer again.

After six months or so, my clinical supervisor at the unit told me about a new role with older adults in a day hospital in Oxford. This meant I had an actual job and could move out from my mother's house. It was dementia on Mondays, Wednesdays and Fridays, and personality disorders on Tuesdays and Thursdays. I was a key worker for a number of patients but at least I wasn't related to any of them. I was still struggling, though. I made strong connections with the patients and their families, but I was frustrated by how little I could do for them. They would all deteriorate and die. I found myself dreaming about my patients. I started running to de-stress. I lost a lot of weight but I didn't lose much stress.

Clouds raced across the face of the volcano. The weather was clearing out just as we too were moving on from Tetebatu. On the perimeter of the nearest field a circle of women had gathered to thresh armfuls of rice. Further out, another woman was weeding, waist-deep in the water. A barefoot old man harvested elephant grass with a parang. I closed the journal. All this reminiscing about the false starts in my career was probably just the end-of-holiday blues. The real reason I was up so early was because I had sense of foreboding. I instinctively knew something had happened last night. I thought about one of my half-sisters who had recently been diagnosed with cancer.

At the Oxford Trust there was a professor of clinical psychology who was starting a project with the Institute of Psychiatry and suggested I should apply for it. That was how I ended up back in south-east London in the big residents' lounges of nursing homes, sitting in the stale air, surrounded by high-backed chairs. I coded the two women in front of the television. I coded the woman sitting opposite me, intent on caressing a piece of cotton handkerchief between her thumbs and forefingers. Now and again, she paused to call out, 'Nurse, nurse, nurse!' Nobody came. I coded an old man staring out of the locked window, always in the same spot, apart from when he recited the Lord's Prayer in the dining room to the delight of the staff. One of the pacers hesitated by the door. She withdrew her hand from the pocket of her long limp cardigan to stroke her fingers over a picture frame as if she had just discovered it. She wandered out of the room, the la-la-la of her echolalia fading down the corridor. A woman yanked her incontinence pad from under her skirt and held it high. She yelled, then let it drop onto the burnt orange carpet where it lay, a sodden nappy.

Around me now, the Tetebatu day was really starting up. Men were firing up a kiln fuelled by chaff to make bricks to finish the row of huts next to ours. One gave me a toothy grin as he carried a stack of bricks on a wooden hod along the path. A pickup truck pulled into the yard behind me. It was time to fill my rucksack and go.

On the lumpy ride to Lombok Airport I was still thinking about dementia mapping. How I'd signed an ethics contract not to intervene unless it was a matter of life and death. How saddened I had been. How it was all a matter of life and death. I had started to dream about those residents too. I tried to cling to the advice of my clinical supervisor. I tried to focus on the purpose of the research: to improve dementia care.

Later, I worked for a while in a general practice surgery in Hampstead Village, one of the smartest parts of London. The surgery was even named after John Keats, the physician who quit medicine for poetry. I was there to offer one-to-one sessions for patients with anxiety, part of a project at University College London. The idea was to use people like me to alleviate pressure on the qualified staff. But nobody in Hampstead wanted to see a 20-something trainee. I was sitting in an empty consulting room listening to the clock. Once again I wasn't actually helping anyone. I found opportunities back at UCL, assisting PhD students with their research.

On the day I finally faced the truth, I took the afternoon off and wandered through London. I stopped for a coffee and a cigarette in Trafalgar Square and then meandered into the Tate Modern. Olafur Eliasson had brought a vast glowing sun into the Turbine Hall using mirrors on the ceiling. A perfect circle, bright in the centre with warm bronze emanating around it. A hazy mist softened the cavernous gallery. People stood in awe or lay on the floor as if in worship. It was like being closer than you could ever be to a sunset. It was like being part of the sunset yourself, part of the sidereal. Even lying on the hard concrete floor, it warmed me. People around me made shapes, captivated in their reflected selves on the ceiling. Each of us alone in our own infinity.

I lay on my back in the Turbine Hall and thought about my longing to be a clinical psychologist. It was the one thing I had wanted for my life since I was 13. It was still as far away as the sun. I admitted that I wasn't right for a life in the National Health Service. For a start, I wasn't 'hardy' enough. Both my parents made that clear. My dad would hang his head whenever I cried in front of him. He would tell me to toughen up. I'd always been sensitive to the emotions of others. My empathy was in constant overdrive. It meant I developed strong bonds with the patients or with their families, but that was never enough. I wanted to make things better for them. I never felt I was doing enough, even when my hands weren't tied by ethics contracts. I couldn't switch off my empathy circuitry. It was all-consuming. I would end up like the woman who quit the high dependency unit in Liverpool. She had gone off to make jewellery in Brighton.

I never qualified as a clinical psychologist. Life had other plans. As if by destiny, early one morning, a few days after lying in the Turbine Hall, I bumped into one of the professors in the university staff kitchen. She said her PhD students had mentioned my name. She said she'd recommend me for a master's degree in work psychology at Aston Business School. By the time I was sitting on a grey plastic seat in the freezing air conditioning at the departure gate in Lombok Airport, all that was ten years behind me. I was a chartered psychologist. I'd recovered from my 'dirty sell-out' career change. As part of an occupational psychology consultancy, I had dived enthusiastically into what Miss Piggy calls, Bizznuss! I had worked with multinational pharmaceutical clients, and even defence manufacturers, and I had just resigned from a global organisational development role at Barclays Bank. I no longer smoked, and I was in a long-term relationship. I fed my helping habit with voluntary work at Smart Works, coaching unemployed women in interview skills. At the finale of the improvisation course, I'd appeared solo on stage. That day at Lombok Airport, despite my early morning foreboding, and the sense that I was continually restarting my career, I was the strongest I had ever been. Then my mobile phone vibrated.

My mother had had a subdural haematoma as a result of a fall. The rest is a blur. Three flights alone as Rod had come out for work and flew back separately via Kuala Lumpur. I zombied through Bali – Jakarta – Dubai – London, airport corridors and the backs of reclined seats. She'd collapsed outside a shop in Witney. After seven hours in brain surgery they discovered another bleed. That meant another two hours. The blur continued. In the intensive care unit, lost in a mass of wires coming from every part of her. Bleeping machines. A place where there is no day or night. Watery coffee in beige plastic cups. Too hot to taste. My Indonesian journal filled itself with medical notes. Hushed conversations with doctors and nurses huddled around her bed. I slept on the thin cushions of the chairs in the narrow visitors' consulting room, the metal frame digging into my ribs. The stain of bad news conversations on the walls. I cancelled my work and moved into her house, obsessively washing her linen and scrubbing the kitchen tiles. I piled up the years of accumulated junk from car boot sales. Rod phoned to ask when I was coming home. I didn't know. When I wasn't hoovering the house or paying her bills, I spent all hours at the hospital, asking questions, taking notes. I was the good daughter again. Once, when I rang the entry phone for the ICU and announced I was there to visit Sylvia Baker, I was asked who I was.

'I'm her mother,' I said.

In a blink I reverted to the role she had always given me. Only her needs mattered. She would never know how many days I sat by her bed. It was as if my whole life was made for this moment. My mother would die of dementia; what did that leave of me? Without her I was nothing.

It wasn't only my mother who fell that day. I had been playing snakes and ladders all my life. There's always a big snake right at the top waiting to swallow you all the way back down to square twenty-four. It took me a couple of years to climb back up again. I started psychotherapy with a woman who knew exactly what to do. Over the next eighteen months she introduced me to my inner child. She took me on a cord-cutting experience to sever the connection with my mother. Fat tubes like ridged vacuum cleaner hoses suctioned on to my belly and chest. When I sliced through them, they grew back like tentacles and reattached themselves. It was a long and messy job. The therapist taught me that my mother's problems weren't mine to solve. She taught me to discover my own values, to figure out what I liked to do. Gradually she helped me build a sense of the real Jess Baker rather than the super-confident projection that I had painstakingly designed to fool so many. Captivated by the idea of self-image, I briefly started a skincare business. Then, appalled by the cosmetics industry, I worked on a book about the Beauty Illusion. Another career crossroads. Another round of snakes and ladders. Another book not written.

In the years after that, I started to build mindfulness practice into my life. I went on courses in self-compassion. I did a lot of work on my inner critic. A lot of forgiving myself. I examined my thinking and let go of some irrational beliefs. I learnt to set boundaries and to sell my services without feeling apologetic for charging. Eventually I began using all this with my clients. I designed the Tame Your Inner Critic online programme. To my surprise, it wasn't just private clients who were interested. Businesses wanted me to talk to their employees about the inner critic, self-sabotage, the imposter syndrome and even the art of helping.

Perhaps you are doing some of this work yourself, following your own story. You might be starting to let go of the role of the compulsive helper. You might be trying to meet your own needs. You might be searching out your true Self. If you are, I'd like to share some thoughts about where I am today, and what helps or hinders me as I try to work towards a compassionate life.

You are likely to have setbacks and face resistance, both internally and externally, but I want to convince you that it's worth the effort to keep going. Believing that has probably been the most important part: trusting that all the hard work will be worth it. By doing that work I've reached a point where I see every situation as an opportunity to dig deeper into my beliefs and motives for helping. These days I know my inner critic so well, I can hear her a mile off. I no longer entertain her. That's why she's sitting on a rock sulking. By developing my self-compassion, I've turned my 4 a.m. fretting into the opportunity for gratitude. I do still sometimes wake early but I no longer spend the time ruminating on the past or fearful about the future. By tackling my own imposter syndrome I've stood in front of large audiences and claimed my accomplishments, to role model what they can do.

The second most important thing after believing you can do it is to ask for help. I finally learnt to do that. I asked for help with this book. That's why it actually got written. You need to choose carefully. Find people you can trust, the ones who are keen to meet your needs rather than just benefit from your help. Otherwise, they may resent the role reversal when you ask something of them. When you do find someone to support you it can be a good idea to enrol them in what you are trying to change. If you already have a friend or partner who complains when you take on too much, you might give them permission to keep doing this. If there's someone you want to confide in, you could agree with them that they will simply listen and resist the impulse to start telling you what to do.

On that note, if you have been reading this book and thinking about someone you know rather than yourself, I'd urge you to reflect on how you can help them. With the best intentions, you might be tempted to pass on your insights. The important thing here is not to launch into offering advice. Telling someone they should let go of their Good Person Belief is likely to be met with puzzlement. Urging them to give up their They-Couldn't-Survive-Without-Me Belief and leave their CS relationship wouldn't go down too well! Instead, consider what form of help they need. Remember the power of supportive help, sometimes just listening is enough. Be honest with yourself: are you maintaining their compulsive helping? How much do you rely on them?

Another source of support can be other helpers you know. They can be a sounding board to remind you that it's okay to look after your own needs when you are helping others – that you don't have to put up with helper's guilt. You could meet up with one or more in a compulsive helper support group – Self-Helpers! You could spend time together sharing what's going well or not so well, in a safe and confidential setting. This would give you the opportunity to help each other maintain a Healthy Helper Mindset.

Begin to recognise when your boundaries alarm system has tripped. Especially the times when you have an opportunity to push back, but don't. You hear yourself saying, 'Here I go again' or 'Why did I just say yes? I really don't have time.' Rather than giving your inner critic airtime, this is a chance to recommit to the changes you are trying to make. Respect your own boundaries: no one else will if you don't. Phone them back and say you can't do it after all. It doesn't make you any less capable. It doesn't make you any less lovely. You are just doing the very thing others are better at: meeting your own needs.

There will be highs and lows; that's the nature of being alive. There will be setbacks, just as there are in learning anything difficult. I still have relapses of compulsive helping. That example of driving past the parking spaces after seeing the widowed neighbour. Hands up. That was me.

Don't try to take everything on at once. Try teeny-tiny steps. Prioritise one or two spotlights or pieces of advice in this survival guide. You can come back and try the others when you are ready. There are always opportunities to take your self-awareness and insights to ever higher levels. Being a healthy helper fills you with energy. That's when you can do your greatest work.

The world needs more helpers like you.

Postscript

There's a final activity my clients do at my 'Hideaways'. I bring along a bag of beautiful postcards collected from art galleries and museum gift shops. I spread these across the table and invite each person to choose one. My clients write a postcard with love to their future self. I gather in the cards and post them back on a date they choose (maybe three months later or on their birthday).

I would like to invite you to do something similar. Write an encouraging letter to your future self. In that letter, remind yourself about any insights you've gained from reading this book. Make a note of one or two spotlights you'd like to come back to. Encourage yourself to review your progress. Tell your future self that you forgive them for any self-criticism they may be experiencing. Reassure yourself that you will overcome any setbacks. Remind yourself to look after your own needs. Congratulate yourself on any progress you've made. Tell yourself to stick with it ... you can do this ... you're amazing ... whatever you feel inspired to write. Seal and self-address the letter, then give it to someone you trust to post it back on a date of your choice.

With love from you.

List of Spotlights

Notes

Authors' Note

p.8   **Stress now accounts for over 30 per cent of sickness absence:** 'NHS Workforce Statistics – October 2020', NHS Digital, 28 Jan 2021 (https://digital.nhs.uk/data-and-information/publications/statistical/nhs-workforce-statistics/october-2020#summary).

p.8   **A US report on 10,000 nurses:** Linda H. Aiken, Sean P. Clarke, Douglas M. Sloane, et al., 'Hospital Nurse Staffing and Patient Mortality, Nurse Burnout, and Job Dissatisfaction', *JAMA* 23(30) (2002), pp.1987–93. There is plenty of evidence of stress in professional carers. For example, in 2016, the Center for Advanced Studies in Child Welfare at the University of Minnesota surveyed 700 child protection workers. They found that 83 per cent reported secondary traumatic stress and 67 per cent felt overwhelmed by their duties.
Kristine Piescher, Traci LaLiberte, Elizabeth Snyder, Sandra Ayoo and Misty Blue, 'Minnesota Child Welfare Workforce Stabilization Study', Center for Advanced Studies in Child Welfare (CASCW) School of Social Work, University of Minnesota (2016).

p.8   **There are around 6.5 million:** According to Carers UK. See 'Carers Week 2020 Research Report', Carers Week, 2020 (www.carersuk.org/images/CarersWeek2020/CW_2020_Research_Report_WEB.pdf).

p.11   **Many amazing helpers have shared their experiences in inter-views and questionnaires:** If you'd like to answer the questionnaire we used or use it for your own research purposes, the latest version can be found at www.jessbaker.co.uk/shs.

p.11   **Driven by the principles of qualitative research:** See, for example, Barney Glaser and Anselm L. Strauss, *The Discovery of Grounded Theory: Strategies for Qualitative Research* (1967, 1999).

Prologue

p.15   **Orangutan mothers:** T.M. Smith, C. Austin, K. Hinde, E.R. Vogel and M. Arora, 'Cyclical nursing patterns in wild orangutans', *Science Advances* 3(5) (2017).
Find out more about orangutans in *Reflections of Eden: My Years with the Orangutans of Borneo*, by Birute Galdikas.

p.16   ***The New York Times* reported that thirty-eight people ignored the cries of Kitty Genovese:** For more on this see 'Bystander Effect' in just about every textbook on Social Psychology, for example, *The Psychology of Prosocial Behaviour*, edited by Stefan Stürmer and Mark Snyder.

p.16   **In his most famous experiment:** J.M. Darley and D. Batson, '"From Jerusalem To Jericho": A Study of Situational and Dispositional Variables in Helping Behavior', *Journal of Personality and Social Psychology* 27(1) (1973), pp.100–8.

Chapter 1: How Can I Help?

p.25   **Creamy coleslaw:** Grated red or white cabbage, celeriac and carrot mixed with mayonnaise, chopped nuts, sultanas, a squeeze of lemon juice and a teaspoon of water.

p.28   **Louis Penner of the Cancer Institute:** L.A. Penner, R.J.W. Cline et al., 'Parents' Empathic Responses and Pain and Distress in Pediatric Patients', *Basic Applied Social Psychology* 30(2) (2008), pp.102–13.

p.36   **The documentary *The Helper* about foreign domestic workers:** See https://helperdocumentary.com (2017).

Chapter 2: Love or Money?

p.39   **A group of scientists have come up with the following formula:** D. Keltner, A. Kogan, P.K. Piff and S.R. Saturn, 'The Sociocultural Appraisals, Values, and Emotions (SAVE) Framework of Prosociality: Core Processes from Gene to Meme', *Annual Review of Psychology* 65 (2014), pp.425–60.

p.41   **Prosocial behaviour evolves where strong reciprocators emerge:** See H. Gintis, S. Bowles, R. Boyd, and E. Fehr, 'Explaining altruistic behaviour in humans' in R. Dunbar and L. Barrett (eds), *The Oxford Handbook of Evolutionary Psychology* (Oxford University Press, 2007).

p.41   **Chimpanzees demonstrate this conformity to social norms:** F. De Waal, 'The Chimpanzee's service economy: Food for grooming', *Evolution and Human Behavior* 18(6) (1997), pp.375–86.

p.44   **Bedrock of morality, the glue of society:** M.L. Hoffman, 'Empathy, Justice and Social Change' in H. Maibom (ed.), *Empathy and Morality* (Oxford University Press, 2014), pp.71–96.

p.44   **The source of everyday miracles:** K.L. Lewis and S.D. Hodges, 'Empathy is Not Always as Personal as You May Think: The Use of Stereotypes in Empathic Accuracy' in J. Decety (ed.) *Empathy: From Bench to Bedside* (MIT Press, 2014), pp.73–84.

p.44   **Any problem immersed in empathy becomes soluble:** S. Baron-Cohen, *Zero Degrees of Empathy* (Penguin, 2012).

p.46   **The same neural circuits involved in the experience of physical pain:** J. Decety and K.J. Michalska, 'How Children Develop Empathy: The Contribution of Developmental Affective Neuroscience' in J. Decety (ed.), *Empathy: From Bench to Bedside* (MIT Press, 2014), pp.167–90.

p.46   **Empathy: a translation of *Einfühlung* – feeling into:** K. Stueber, 'Empathy' in Edward N. Zalta (ed.), *The Stanford Encyclopedia of Philosophy* (Metaphysics Research Lab, Stanford University, 2019).

p.46   **Emotional contagion:** See a useful review in E. Hatfield, R.L. Rapson and Y-C. L. Le, 'Emotional Contagion and Empathy' in J. Decety and W. Ickes (eds), *The Social Neuroscience of Empathy* (MIT Press, 2019).

p.46   **Cognitive and emotional empathy inhabit two separate brain systems:** J. Zaki and K. Ochsner, 'The Cognitive Neuroscience of Sharing and Understanding Others' Emotions' in J. Decety (ed.), *Empathy: From Bench to Bedside* (MIT Press, 2014), pp.207–26.

p.47   **The students listened to a fake interview with a terminally ill girl, Sheri Summers:** See Daniel Batson, *A Scientific Search for Altruism* (Oxford University Press, 2019).

p.48　**A lot of the work that is done in global health:** To clarify, Melanie Wendland was advocating emotional empathy as well as cognitive empathy. During our interview she made this clear, for example when she stressed that a researcher should 'allow the feelings to come and empathise'. Or when she said, 'Nurses and doctors have a lot of empathy but they put that in their side pocket, and my role as a designer is to help them reconnect with their own empathy.' I wish there was space in the text to quote more of her interview.

p.49　**Eudaimonistic judgement:** 'Eudaimonism' translates roughly from the Greek as 'wellbeing'.

p.49　**The first two of her requirements for compassion she takes directly from Aristotle:** From *The Art of Rhetoric*, though his term '*eleos*' is usually translated as 'pity' rather than 'compassion'. Aristotle's definition is: 'Let pity then, be a certain pain occasioned by an apparently destructive evil or pain's occurring to one who does not deserve it, which the pitier might expect to suffer himself or that one of his own would, and this whenever it should seem near at hand.'

p.50　**Judgements of fault are jostled by a crowd of factors:** Many of those factors are picked up by the SAVE formula, as previously mentioned. See D. Keltner, A. Kogan, P.K. Piff and S.R. Saturn, 'The Sociocultural Appraisals, Values, and Emotions (SAVE) Framework of Prosociality: Core Processes from Gene to Meme', *Annual Review of Psychology* 65 (2014), pp.425–60.

p.50　**Jean Decety had people watch videos of AIDS sufferers:** J. Decety, S. Echols and J. Correll, 'The Blame Game: The Effect of Responsibility and Social Stigma on Empathy for Pain', *Journal of Cognitive Neuroscience* 22(5) (2010), pp.985–97.

Chapter 3: The Unhealthy Helper

p.59 **A charity that makes wigs for children undergoing cancer treatment:** Little Princess Trust (www.littleprincesses.org.uk).

p.59 **One of her photographs of her father with dementia was shortlisted for an award:** Lucy Williams Photography (www.lucywilliamsphotography.co.uk/dads-dementia).

p.60 **Helgeson refers to this as 'unmitigated communion':** V.S. Helgeson and H.L. Fritz, 'A Theory of Unmitigated Communion', *Personality and Social Psychology Review* 2(3) (1998), pp.173–83.
V.S. Helgeson, J. Swanson, et al., 'Links between unmitigated communion, interpersonal behaviors and well-being: A daily diary approach', *Journal of Research in Personality* 57 (2015), pp.53–60.

p.60 **Building on a theory first proposed by David Bakan in the 1960s:** See D. Bakan, *The Duality of Human Existence* (Beacon, 1966).

p.63 **Pathological Altruism:** This term was originally coined by the psychoanalyst Nancy McWilliams in her article, 'The Psychology of the Altruist', *Psychoanalytic Psychology* 1(3) (1984), pp.193–213.

p.63 **National Association of Social Workers code of conduct:** www.socialworkers.org/About/Ethics/Code-of-Ethics/Code-of-Ethics-English.

p.63 **American Nurses Association Code of Ethics:** As quoted in William Steele's *Reducing Compassion Fatigue, Secondary Traumatic Stress, and Burnout* (Routledge, 2019).

p.65 **'You feel really guilty because you're not giving people the care that they fundamentally need':** I heard similar accounts from clinical professionals making difficult decisions regarding patients' care. I didn't

quite know how to categorise this theme until a specialist nurse called it 'moral distress'. Philosopher Andrew Jameton first described it as the psychological unease 'of being in a situation in which one is constrained from acting on what one knows to be right'. A report by the British Medical Association explains it as a result of having 'a lack of power or agency, or structural limitations, such as insufficient staff, resources, training or time'. Professor Alison Leary, an expert in workforce modelling in healthcare, told me, 'It's like they've promised themselves they should do their job well and they can't meet those expectations. And these people are everywhere.'
A. Jameton, *Nursing Practice: The Ethical Issues* (Prentice Hall, 1984).
'Moral distress and moral injury: Recognising and tackling it for UK doctors', British Medical Association, 30 November 2021 (www.bma.org.uk/media/4209/bma-moral-distress-injury-survey-report-june-2021.pdf).

p.66   **Job adverts for child protection staff:** See L. van Dernoot Lipsky, *Trauma Stewardship: An Everyday Guide to Caring for Self While Caring for Others* (Berrett-Koehler, 2009).

p.66   **Karen Saakvitne and Laurie Pearlman, two of the leading researchers in this area, have urged employers that they have a 'duty to warn' applicants:** As mentioned by Charles R. Figley (ed.) in *Treating Compassion Fatigue* (Routledge, 2002), p.189.

p.66   **The recent initiative of compassionate leadership in the health service in the UK:** See King's Fund (www.kingsfund.org.uk/projects/changing-culture-collective-leadership). For more on compassionate leadership, see https://jessbaker.co.uk/compassionate-leader/.

Chapter 4: Irrational Beliefs

p.75   **Neurons start firing in a matter of milliseconds:** See A. Damasio, *The Feeling of What Happens* (Vintage, 2000).

p.78 **That's the amygdala in action:** See A. Damasio, *Self Comes to Mind: Constructing the Conscious Brain* (Vintage, 2012).

p.79 **A woman, both of whose amygdalae were calcified:** See A. Damasio, *The Feeling of What Happens* (Vintage, 2000).

p.79 **We spend as much as a quarter of our lives listening to our inner voice:** C.L. Heavey and R.T. Hurlburt, 'The Phenomena of Inner Experience', *Consciousness and Cognition* 17(3) (2008), pp.798–810.

p.80 **Decentering:** J.C. Watson and L.S. Greenberg, 'Empathic Resonance: A Neuroscience Perspective' in J. Decety and W. Ickes (eds), *The Social Neuroscience of Empathy* (MIT Press, 2009), pp.125–38.

p.84 **The Science of Mindset:** World Economic Forum, *The Science of How Mindset Transforms the Human Experience*, Alia Crum, 21 February 2018 [Video], YouTube (www.youtube.com/watch?v=vTDYtwqKBI8).

p.84 **She studied housekeeping staff in seven US hotels:** A.J. Crum and E.J. Langer, 'Mind-set Matters: Exercise and the Placebo Effect', *Psychological Science* 18(2) (2007), pp.165–71.

p.84 **Mind over Milkshakes study:** A.J. Crum, W.R Corbin, K.D. Brownell and P. Salovey, 'Mind Over Milkshakes', *Health Psychology* 30(4) (2011), pp.424–29.

p.86 **This has been called the avoidance mindset. Neuroscientists have used imaging techniques to show that this is associated with a different area of the brain:** R.J. Davidson, 'What does the prefrontal cortex "do" in affect: perspectives on frontal EEG asymmetry research', *Biological Psychology* 67 (2004), pp.219–33.

Chapter 5: The Good Person Belief

p.91   **Da! Da! Da!:** The three Da! refer to '*damyata*', '*dayadhvam*', and '*datta*', which roughly translate as 'self-control', 'give', and 'be compassionate'.

p.110   **This involves various types of meditation. There's a growing body of evidence to show that they can bring health benefits:** See M. Williams and D. Penman, *Mindfulness* (Piatkus, 2011).

Chapter 6: The Help Everyone Belief

p.122   **They have found a sizeable genetic component, especially for emotional empathy, estimated at 68 per cent in one study:** M.H. Davis, C. Luce and S.J. Kraus, 'The Heritability of Characteristics Associated with Dispositional Empathy', *Journal of Personality and Social Psychology* 62 (1994), pp.369–91.

p.122   **A heap of evidence that helping has a hereditary component:** D. Keltner, A. Kogan, P.K. Piff and S.R. Saturn, 'The Sociocultural Appraisals, Values, and Emotions (SAVE) Framework of Prosociality: Core Processes from Gene to Meme', *Annual Review of Psychology* 65 (2014), pp.425–60.

Chapter 7: They Couldn't Survive Without Me

p.144   **280,000 people who care for someone with dementia twenty-four hours a day:** According to dementiacarers.org.uk.

p.147 **Although some have criticised her for being anecdotal or unsci-entific:** M. McGrath and B. Oakley, 'Codependency and Pathological Altruism' in B. Oakley, A. Knafo, G. Madhavan and B.S. Wilson (eds), *Pathological Altruism* (Oxford University Press, 2012).

p.148 **Dependent Personality Disorder is defined as:** For fuller descriptions of each of the personality disorders, see A.T. Beck, D.D. Davis and A. Freeman (eds), *Cognitive Therapy of Personality Disorders* (Guilford Press, 2015).
And T.A. Widiger (ed.), *The Oxford Handbook of Personality Disorders* (Oxford University Press, 2012), pp.505–26.
Or for a psychoanalytic perspective, see N. McWilliams, *Psychoanalytic Diagnosis* (Guilford Press, 2011).

Chapter 8: The No Needs Belief

p.167 **'It's flipping hard work sometimes':** This didn't come from the interviews or questionnaire respondents. It was a response from a man on Twitter to a post about being a mediator. It summed up what many had said.

p.170 **This can block personal growth and the formation of an autonomous identity:** C. Zahn-Waxler and C. Van Hulle, 'Empathy, Guilt, and Depression: When Caring for Others Becomes Costly to Children' in B. Oakley, A. Knafo, G. Madhavan and B.S. Wilson (eds), *Pathological Altruism* (Oxford University Press, 2012), p.321–44.

Chapter 9: The Healthy Helper Mindset

p.180   **Tend and befriend:** S.E. Taylor, 'Tend and Befriend Theory', in A.M. van Lange, A.W. Kruglanski and E.T. Higgins (eds), *Handbook of Theories of Social Psychology* (SAGE Publications, 2012).

p.180   **Women are more prepared to talk through their stress with women friends:** S.E. Taylor, L. Cousino Klein, B.P. Lewis, T.L. Gruenewald, R.A.R. Gurung and J.A. Updegraff, 'Biobehavioral Responses to Stress in Females: Tend-and-Befriend, Not Fight-or-Flight', *Psychological Review* 107(3) (2000), pp.411–29.

p.180   **Higher levels of oxytocin found in women:** D. Marazziti, S. Baroni, F. Mucci, et al., 'Sex-Related Differences in Plasma Oxytocin Levels in Humans', *Clinical Practice & Epidemiology in Mental Health* 15 (2019), pp.58–63.

p.181   **Keltner and his colleagues pointed out that, 'emerging evidence suggests that acting with kindness yields many kinds of benefits for the giver':** D. Keltner, A. Kogan, P.K. Piff and S.R. Saturn, 'The Sociocultural Appraisals, Values, and Emotions (SAVE) Framework of Prosociality: Core Processes from Gene to Meme', *Annual Review of Psychology* 65 (2014), pp.425–60.

p.181   **It can have a quiet word with the amygdala:** G. Domes, M. Heinrichs, J. Glascher, et al., 'Oxytocin Attenuates Amygdala Responses to Emotional Faces Regardless of Valence', *Biological Psychiatry* 62(10) (2007), pp.1187–90.

p.182   **Public health expert Doug Oman reported that 'volunteering is associated on average with longer life, better self-rated health, and better physical functioning':** D. Oman, C.E. Thoresen, C.E. and K. McMahon, 'Volunteerism and Mortality Among the Community-Dwelling Elderly', *Journal of Health Psychology* 4(3) (1999), pp.301–16 quoted in S.G. Post (ed.) *Altruism and Health* (Oxford University Press, 2007).

p.183 **Shelley Taylor, has also written a review paper on social support:** S.E. Taylor, 'Social Support: A Review' in Howard S. Friedman (ed.), *The Oxford Handbook of Health Psychology* (Oxford University Press, 2011).

p.189 **Marie Kondo is the guru of the joy of folding things up really small:** See one of her many videos: Marie Kondo, *The KonMari Fold | Basics*, 25 April 2020 [Video], YouTube (www.youtube.com/watch?v=IjkmqbJTLBM).

p.189 **Psychology of happiness:** See, for example, M. Seligman, *Flourish: A New Understanding of Happiness and Well-Being* (Nicholas Brealey Publishing, 2011).

p.192 **When we find meaning in our work:** See various sources on positive psychology, for example, Martin Seligman's book *Flourish: A New Understanding of Happiness and Well-Being* (Nicholas Brealey Publishing, 2011).

Chapter 10: The Hardy Helper

p.205 **The term was first taken up by Suzanne Kobasa:** S.C. Kobasa, 'Stressful life events, personality, and health: An inquiry into hardiness', *Journal of Personality and Social Psychology* 37(1) (1979), pp.1–11.

p.205 **The Bell Telephone study inspired a wealth of research showing the advantages of hardiness:** See S.J. Stein and P.T. Bartone, *Hardiness* (Wiley, 2020) for a review.

p.205 **Norwegian police trainees:** A. Sandvik, E. Gjevestad, E. Aabrekk, P. Øhman, P-L Kjendlie, S.W. Hystad, P. Bartone, A. Hansen and B. Johnsen, 'Physical fitness and psychological hardiness as predictors of parasympathetic control in response to stress: A Norwegian police simulator training study', *Journal of Police and Criminal Psychology* 35 (2019), pp.504–17.

p.205 Another study in Norway tracked hundreds of nurses over a two-year period: I. Saksvik-Lehouillier, B. Bjorvatn, N. Magerøy and S. Pallesen, 'Hardiness, psychosocial factors and shift work tolerance among nurses – a 2-year follow-up study', *Journal of Advanced Nursing* 72(8) (2016), pp.1800–12.

p.205 In Morocco, hardiness profiles were collected from nurses and doctors: H. Chtibi, A. Ahami, F.Z. Azzaoui, A. Khadmaoui, K. Mammad and F. Elmassioui, 'Study of Psychological Resilience Among Health Care Professionals in Ibn Sina Hospital, Rabat, Morocco', *Open Journal of Medical Psychology* 7(3) (2018), pp.47–57.

p.206 Gallows humour: A useful review of gallows humour in different settings can be found in S. Christopher, 'An Introduction to Black Humour as a Coping Mechanism for Student Paramedics', *Journal of Paramedic Practice* 7(12) (2015).

p.206 Firefighters in Los Angeles: See 'One Way that Firefighters Cope with Stress' in S.J. Stein and P.T. Bartone, *Hardiness* (Wiley, 2020), pp.182–83.

p.206 It can promote physiological thriving: See R.A. Dienstbier, 'Arousal and physiological toughness: Implications for mental and physical health', *Psychological Review* 96(1) (1989), pp.84–100.
And also E.S. Epel, B.S. McEwen and J.R. Ickovics, 'Embodying psychological thriving: Physical thriving in response to stress', *Journal of Social Issues* 54(2) (1998), pp.301–22.

p.207 Scientists from the University of Barcelona studied Catalans bungee jumping off a bridge: J. Castellà, J. Boned, J.L. Ulrich and A. Sanz, 'Jump and free fall! Memory, attention, and decision-making processes in an extreme sport', *Cognition and Emotion* 34(2) (2020), pp.262–72.

p.207 Navy SEALs: E.N. Smith, M.D. Young and A.J. Crum, 'Stress, Mindsets, and Success in Navy SEALs Special Warfare Training', *Frontiers in Psychology* 10(2962) (2020), pp.1–11.

p.207 **Mindset interventions:** You can view the Stanford Mind & Body Lab Stress Intervention videos at https://mbl.stanford.edu/interventions-toolkits/rethink-stress-intervention.

p.207 **Crum studied a group of employees at UBS:** A.J. Crum, P. Salovey and S. Achor, 'Evaluating a Mindset Training Program to Unleash the Enhancing Nature of Stress', *Academy of Management Proceedings* (2011).

p.209 **Compassion satisfaction:** B.H. Stamm, 'Measuring Compassion Satisfaction as Well as Fatigue: Developmental History of the Compassion Satisfaction and Fatigue Test' in C.R. Figley (ed.), *Treating Compassion Fatigue* (Routledge, 2002).
Also see the Compassion Satisfaction & Compassion Fatigue Test (PROQOL V5), which is available to complete free online.

p.210 **Post-traumatic growth:** E.G. Tedeschi and L.G. Calhoun, 'Posttraumatic Growth: Conceptual Foundations and Empirical Evidence', *Psychological Enquiry* 15(1) (2004), pp.1–18.

Chapter 11: The Compassionate Life

p.224 **As I try to work towards a compassionate life:** The compassionate life, as referred to in this chapter, is an attempt to integrate the three types of compassion mentioned elsewhere in the book (self-compassion, compassion as a motivator to help, and the compassionate perspective). The compassionate life would be the ultimate goal for compassionate people, and is probably what is most lacking in this world today. For more on this see https://jessbaker.co.uk/the-compassionate-life/.

Select Bibliography

Adler, A., *Understanding Life: An Introduction to the Psychology of Alfred Adler* (Oneworld, 1927/1997).

American Psychiatric Association, *Diagnostic and Statistical Manual of Mental Disorders*, 5th ed. (DSM 5) (American Psychiatric Association, 2013).

Aristotle, *The Art of Rhetoric* (Penguin, 1991).

Bakan, D., *The Duality of Human Existence* (Beacon, 1966).

Baron-Cohen, S., *The Essential Difference: Men, Women, and the Extreme Male Brain* (Penguin, 2003).

Baron-Cohen, S., *Zero Degrees of Empathy: A New Theory of Human Cruelty and Kindness* (Penguin, 2012).

Batson, C.D., *A Scientific Search for Altruism: Do We Only Care About Ourselves?* (Oxford University Press, 2019).

Beattie, M., *Codependent No More: How to Stop Controlling Others and Start Caring for Yourself* (Hazelden Publishing, 1986).

Beck, A.T., *Cognitive Therapy and the Emotional Disorders* (Penguin, 1976).

Beck, A.T., Davis, D.D., and Freeman, A. (eds), *Cognitive Therapy of Personality Disorders* (Guilford Press, 2015).

Berry, C.R., *When Helping You Is Hurting Me: Escaping the Messiah Trap* (Crossroads, 2003).

Bloom, P., *Against Empathy: The Case for Rational Compassion* (Vintage, 2018).

Bridges, W., *Transitions: Making Sense of Life's Changes* (Perseus Books, 1979/2019).

Brown, B., *Dare to Lead: Brave Work. Tough Conversations. Whole Hearts.* (Vermillion, 2018).

Burns, D., *Feeling Good: The New Mood Therapy* (Harper, 1999).

Burns, D., *The Feeling Good Handbook* (Plume, 1999).

Criado-Perez, C., *Invisible Women: Data Bias in a World Designed for Men* (Vintage, 2019).

Damasio, A., *Descartes' Error: Emotion, Reason and the Human Brain* (Vintage, 1994).

Damasio, A., *Self Comes to Mind: Constructing the Conscious Brain* (Vintage, 2012).

Darwin, C., *On the Origin of Species* (Penguin Classics, 1859/2009).

Davies, S., *Laughology: Improve Your Life with the Science of Laughter* (Crown House Publishing, 2013).

Dawkins, R., *The Extended Selfish Gene* (Oxford University Press, 2016).

Decety, J. (ed.), *Empathy: From Bench to Bedside* (MIT Press, 2014).

De Waal, F., *Mama's Last Hug: Animal Emotions and What They Teach Us About Ourselves* (Granta, 2019).

Dickens, C., *Bleak House* (Penguin, 1852/2003).

Dryden, W., *Rational Emotive Behaviour Therapy* (Routledge, 2015).

Dunbar, R., and Barrett, L. (eds), *The Oxford Handbook of Evolutionary Psychology* (Oxford University Press, 2007).

Ellis, A., *The Myth of Self-Esteem: How Rational Emotive Behaviour Therapy Can Change Your Life Forever* (Prometheus, 2005).

Ellis, A., and MacLaren, C., *Rational Emotive Behaviour Therapy: A Therapist's Guide* (Impact, 2005).

Figley, C.R (ed.), *Treating Compassion Fatigue* (Routledge, 2002).

Galdikas, B.M., *Reflections of Eden: My Years with the Orangutans of Borneo* (Little, Brown & Co, 1995).

Germer, C., and Neff, K., *Teaching the Mindful Self-Compassion Programme* (The Guilford Press, 2019).

Gilbert, P., *The Compassionate Mind* (Constable, 2009).

Glasser, W., *Choice Theory: A New Psychology of Personal Freedom* (Harper Collins, 1998).

Graves, R., *The Greek Myths* (Penguin, 1960/1992).

Hartman, R.S., *The Structure of Value* (Wipf and Stock, 1967).

Hartman, R.S., *Freedom to Live: The Robert Hartman Story* (Wipf and Stock, 1994).

Hauck, P.A., *Overcoming the Rating Game: Beyond Self-Love – Beyond Self-Esteem* (Westminster John Knox Press, 1992).

Heron, J., *Helping the Client: A Creative Practical Guide* (SAGE Publications, 2001).

Hesiod, *Theogony and Works and Days*, translated by M.L. West (Oxford University Press, 1988).

Hobbes, T., *Leviathan* (Cambridge University Press, 1651/1991).

Horney, K., *Neurosis and Human Growth: The Struggle Toward Self-Realization* (W.W. Norton, 1950).

Johnstone, K., *Impro for Storytellers* (Faber and Faber, 1999).

Kant, I., *Critique of Pure Reason* (Penguin Classics, 1781/2007).

Kishimi, I., and Koga, F., *The Courage to be Disliked: How to free yourself, change your life and achieve real happiness* (Allen & Unwin, 2018).

Kohn, A., *The Brighter Side of Human Nature* (Basic Books, 1990).

Korzybski, A., *Selections from Science and Sanity* (Institute of General Semantics, 1948).

Laërtius, D., *Lives of the Eminent Philosophers*, J. Miller (ed.) (Oxford University Press, 2018).

Lakoff, G., and Johnson, M., *Metaphors We Live By* (University of Chicago Press, 1980).

Lichterman, G., *28 Days: What Your Cycle Reveals about Your Moods, Health and Potential* (Adams Media Corporation, 2005).

Luks, A., and Payne, P., *The Healing Power of Doing Good: The Health and Spiritual Benefits of Helping Others* (iUniverse.com, 1991).

Lyubomirsky, S., *The How of Happiness: A New Approach to Getting the Life You Want* (Penguin, 2008).

McBride, K., *Will I Ever Be Good Enough? Healing the Daughters of Narcissistic Mothers* (Atria Books, 2009).

MacFarquhar, L., *Strangers Drowning: Grappling with Impossible Idealism, Drastic Choices, and the Overpowering Urge to Help* (Penguin, 2015).

McGonigal, K., *The Upside of Stress: Why Stress Is Good for You, and How to Get Good at It* (Penguin, 2015).

McGonigal, K., *The Joy of Movement: How exercise helps us find happiness, hope, connection and courage* (Avery, 2019).

McWilliams, N., *Psychoanalytic Diagnosis: Understanding Personality Structure in the Clinical Process* (Guilford Press, 2011).

Maddi, S.R., *Hardiness: Turning Stressful Circumstances into Resilient Growth* (Springer, 2012).

Mandeville, B., *The Fable of the Bees* (Penguin Classics, 1724/1970).

Manne, K., *Down Girl: The Logic of Misogyny* (Penguin, 2018).

Mauss, M., *The Gift: The Form and Reason for Exchange in Archaic Societies*, translated by W.D. Halls (W.W. Norton, 1950/1990).

Monroe, K.R., *The Heart of Altruism: Perceptions of a Common Humanity* (Princeton University Press, 1996).

Neff, K., *Self-Compassion: The Proven Power of Being Kind to Yourself* (William Morrow, 2011).

Nietzsche, F., *Thus Spoke Zarathustra* (Penguin Classics, 1884/1961).

Nietzsche, F., *Beyond Good and Evil* (Penguin, 1886/2003).

Nussbaum, M.C., *Upheavals of Thought: The Intelligence of Emotions* (Cambridge University Press, 2001).

Oakley, B., Knafo, A., Madhavan, G., and Wilson, B.S. (eds), *Pathological Altruism* (Oxford University Press, 2012).

Panda, S., *The Circadian Code: Lose Weight, Supercharge Your Energy and Sleep Well Every Night* (Vermillion, 2018).

Pinker, S., *Enlightenment Now: The Case for Reason, Science, Humanism, and Progress* (Penguin, 2018).

Post, S.G., and Neimark, J., *Why Good Things Happen to Good People: How to Live a Longer, Healthier, Happier Life by the Simple Act of Giving* (Broadway Books, 2007).

Riso, D.R., *Enneagram Transformations: Releases and Affirmations for Healing Your Personality Type* (HarperOne, 1993).

Riso, D.R., and Hudson, R., *Personality Types: Using the Enneagram for Self-Discovery* (HarperOne, 1996).

Rothschild, B., *Help for the Helper: The Psychophysiology of Compassion Fatigue and Vicarious Trauma* (W.W. Norton, 2006).

Schein, E., *Helping* (Berrett-Koehler, 2009).

Schwartz, B., *The Battle for Human Nature: Science, Morality and Modern Life* (W.W. Norton, 1986).

Shriver, L., *We Need to Talk about Kevin* (Serpent's Tail, 2003).

Siegel, D.J., *The Developing Mind: How Relationships and the Brain Interact to Shape Who We Are* (The Guilford Press, 2020).

Smith, A., *The Theory of Moral Sentiments* (Penguin Classics, 1759/2009).

Staub, E., *The Roots of Goodness and Resistance to Evil: Inclusive Caring, Moral Courage, Altruism Born of Suffering, Active Bystandership, and Heroism* (Oxford University Press, 2015).

Steele, W., *Reducing Compassion Fatigue, Secondary Traumatic Stress, and Burnout: A Trauma-Sensitive Workbook* (Routledge, 2019).

Stein, S.J., and Bartone, P.T., *Hardiness: Making Stress Work for You to Achieve Your Life Goals* (Wiley, 2020).

Storr, W., *The Status Game: On Social Position and How We Use It* (William Collins, 2021).

Stürmer, S., and Snyder, M. (eds), The *Psychology of Prosocial Behaviour* (Wiley, 2010).

Tillich, P., *The Courage to Be* (Yale University Press, 1952).

Tillich, P., *The New Being* (University of Nebraska Press, 1955).

Tresilian, J., *How You Feel: The Story of the Mind as Told by the Body* (Robinson, 2020).

Van Dernoot Lipsky, L., *Trauma Stewardship: An Everyday Guide to Caring for Self While Caring for Others* (Berrett-Koehler, 2009).

Walton, G.M., and Crum, A.J. (eds), *Handbook of Wise Interventions: How Social Psychology Can Help People Change* (The Guilford Press, 2021)

Watson, C., *The Courage to Care: A Call for Compassion* (Chatto & Windus, 2020).

Williams, M., and Penman, D., *Mindfulness: A Practical Guide to Finding Peace in a Frantic World* (Piatkus, 2011).

Wilson, L., *Lois Remembers* (Al-Anon Family Group Headquarters Inc., 1979).

Acknowledgements

Little in life is done without help. Not least the writing of a book about helping. With that in mind, we would like to give back warm thanks to all those who have offered us information, resources, expertise and, most importantly, support over the last couple of years.

Foremost are the many people who generously made themselves available to be interviewed or to answer questionnaires about their lives as helpers. This book would not be possible without them. Their honesty, openness and humility were inspiring. We hope that by sharing their stories, others will see that they are not alone. We'd love to acknowledge them more publicly, but many of them are not the sort of people who willingly draw attention to themselves, and we promised to protect their identities. To that end, names and some other identifying features have been changed, or removed, and in a couple of instances situations have been merged. You know who you are. Thank you.

Huge thanks also go out to the many helpers Jess has met through her coaching work. Getting to know them over time has been a privilege. Again, special thanks to those who generously allowed us to share their (disguised) stories.

Thanks to those who read and gave us feedback on (embarrassingly bad) earlier versions of the manuscript: Syma Brown, Carrie Armstrong, Jay Armstrong, Steve and Catherine Petherick, Alice Petherick and Susannah Rickards.

We also offer our thanks to the people who gave us encouragement or advice. In particular: Zachary Pressey, Alison Hopkins, Nicki Credland, Dr Claudia Brown, Matthew Trustman, Professor James Tresilian, Melanie Wendland, Gabrielle Lichterman, Steve Hulland, Ziggy Jackson, Stephanie Davies, Professor Alison Leary, Jigna Dave, Steve O'Neill, Matthew Vincent, Adam Vincent, Jon Da Souza, Suzi Witt.

And to everyone at Graham Maw Christie Agency, especially Maddy Belton and Jane Graham Maw. And to all at Flint Books, especially our editor, Jo de Vries. We were so fortunate to work with someone who deeply understood what we were trying to do in this book from the outset.

In the Acknowledgements section it's conventional to thank your long-suffering partner for putting up with you. In this case, we have long suffered together. We have been holed up in our summer house in the garden for months. At one point we looked down at the hands on the desk in front of us – Jess was on keyboard while Rod was symbiotically wielding the mouse. There have been tears. There's been laughter. It's been exhausting. It's been a joy. We acknowledge each other.

Index

Note: *italicised* page references are illustrations